Hitler Warned Us

At the Obersee near Berchtesgaden. (See p. v)

Hitler Warned Us

The Nazis' Master Plan for a Master Race

JOHN LAFFIN

Brassey's
London • Washington

Also from Brassey's:

CONNAUGHTON
Celebration of Victory: V-E Day 1945

DAVID
Mutiny at Salerno: An Injustice Exposed

FRIEDRICH & VANEGAS
Hitler's Prisoners: Seven Cell Mates Tell Their Stories

LAFFIN
Brassey's Battles: 3,500 Years of Conflict, Campaigns and Wars from A-Z

PROBERT
The Forgotten Air Force: The Royal Air Force in the War Against Japan 1941–1945

GOLDSTEIN ET AL
Rain of Ruin: A Photographic History of Hiroshima and Nagasaki

First English Edition 1995

UK editorial offices: Brassey's, 33 John Street, London WC 1N 2AT
UK orders: Marston Book Services, PO Box 87, Oxford OX2 0DT

North American Orders: Brassey's Inc., PO Box 960,
Herndon, VA 22070, USA

John Laffin has asserted his moral right to be identified as
the author of this work.

Library of Congress Cataloging in Publication Data
available

British Library Cataloguing in Publication Data
A catalogue record for this book is available from the British Library

ISBN 1 85753 103 5 Flexicover

Typeset by M Rules
Printed in Great Britain by The Bath Press, Bath

21.95

Contents

Frontispiece: At the Obersee near Berchtesgaden.

This carefully posed photograph, the only full page photo in *Adolf Hitler* (see p. 3), is profoundly significant in what it says about Hitler the man and Hitler the Führer. Here is the mystic, brooding thinker, the man of destiny, the leader of steel, drawing strength from his beloved Alps. The young man in the background is the perfect Aryan, the German of pure blood with all the finest virtues of the ancient Romans and Spartans. We can be sure that Hitler, Goebbels, the photographer Hoffman and Hitler's intimates studied hundreds of photos of Nazi 'specimens' to find a young man with firmly set shoulders and strong, clearcut features; the jaw and forehead and the fair hair are specially prominent. Even so, there are several signs of retouching to the features of both men and to the rocks that link the older and wiser leader to the thoughtful younger follower in his physical prime. The swastika on the armband has been given special prominence; uniform regulations required it to be 'looking' left but here it has been turned boldly square-on to the camera. Hitler himself and his young Brownshirt are looking into the future which, in 1936, seemed full of hope. This photographic creation could be a composite of three – Hitler and part of the rocky outcrop, the young man and part of the rock, with the lake and mountains brushed in.

By the Same Author

Middle East Journey

Return to Glory

One Man's War

The Walking Wounded

Digger (The Story of the Australian Soldier)

Jackboot (The Story of the German Soldier)

Jack Tar (The Story of the English Seaman)

Tommy Atkins (The Story of the British Soldier)

Swifter Than Eagles (Biography of Marshal of the Royal Air Force Sir John Salmond)

The Face of War

British Campaign Medals

Codes and Ciphers

Boys in Battle

Women in Battle

Anzacs at War

Links of Leadership (Thirty Centuries of Command)

Surgeons in the Field

Americans in Battle

Letters From the Front 1914–18

The French Foreign Legion

Damn the Dardanelles! (The Agony of Gallipoli)

The Australian Army at War 1899–1975

The Arab Armies of the Middle East Wars 1948–1973

The Israeli Army in the Middle East Wars 1948–1973

Fight for the Falklands!

The War of Desperation: Lebanon 1982–85

The Man the Nazis Couldn't Catch

On the Western Front

Brassey's Battles (3,500 Years of Conflict)

Holy War (Islam Fights)

Soldiers of Scotland

Battlefield Archaeology

Western Front 1916–17 – The Price of Honour

Western Front 1917–18 – The Cost of Victory

World War I in Postcards

Greece, Crete & Syria 1941 (The Australian Campaigns)

Secret and Special (Australian Operations)

British Butchers & Bunglers of WWI

The World in Conflict

War Annual 1

War Annual 2

War Annual 3

War Annual 4

War Annual 5

War Annual 6

Western Front Illustrated

Guide to Australian Battlefields of the Western Front 1916–18

Panorama of the Western Front

Digging up the Diggers' War

Forever Forward

Aussie Guide to Britain

Companion to the Western Front

The Arab Mind

The Israeli Mind

Fedayeen: The Arab–Israeli Dilemma

The Dagger of Islam

The Arabs as Master Slavers

The PLO Connections

Know the Middle East

The Hunger to Come

The Anatomy of Captivity

Dictionary of Africa Since 1960

And other titles

Author's Foreword

Adolf Hitler caused me to waste five years of my life. In common with millions of other young men from the countries that became 'The Allies', I spent five years in the army during the war of 1939–45. Certainly I was there of my own free will, as a volunteer, but B.H. (Before Hitler) had no intention of following a Services career.

Many of my friends did not survive the war, some of the 30,000,000 people who lost their lives as a result of a period of international insanity begun by Hitler. It incorporated 'The Holocaust', the obscene genocide of the Jews, and the torture and murder of countless other people considered by the Nazis to be 'inferior' or 'impure'.

Hitler and the Nazis occupied much of our attention, those of us who grew up during the 1920s and 1930s. They were mentioned in the radio news almost daily and they were often the lead item on newsreel programmes that preceded the films showing at the local cinemas. All over the world newspapers filled miles of column inches with reports about Hitler and the other fascist leaders of the day, Mussolini of Italy and Franco of Spain.

Film directors often made Hitler and Mussolini seem to be clown-like figures. The great comedian Charles Chaplin exploited this perception of Hitler in his famous farce, *The Great Dictator*. Many a schoolboy provoked an easy laugh with a Hitler impersonation. He pulled a hank of hair over his forehead, gave himself a charcoal moustache and raised his right hand in a mocking imitation of the Nazi salute. 'Heil Hitler!' everybody shouted amid laughter. I had a friend who developed an amusing skit about Adolf and he was still amusing his mates with it when an Afrika Korps tank shell blew off his head in 1942.

There was nothing funny about Hitler whatsoever. The man had no sense of humour and the Germany of his time was a dark and desperate place, riven with hatreds and prejudices, phobias and resentments.

On reflection, those of us growing up during the 1920s and 1930s, the formative years of the Nazi Germany, were very minor players in one of the great dramas of history. It was a drama of danger and death, of violence and viciousness, of suffering and destruction. And most of it can be laid against the warped mind of one man, Adolf Hitler.

For me as a curious historian, what Hitler did is not as interesting as *how* he was able to do it. His achievements, though perverted, were amazing in their scope. In the end, in a prodigious struggle to defeat Hitler and his allies which ended 50 years ago, the world very nearly destroyed itself in wiping out Hitler and his Nazis.

The Hitler enigma has always interested me. With access to some unusual sources, I have attempted to show in this book the methods by which Hitler gained power, how he exploited it and how he either deceived or terrified his internal and external opponents into submission. I show the depths of his extraordinary influence on his German contemporaries by revealing what they were saying about this 'saviour and redeemer', this 'Divine Being', and how he usually presented himself to them. Could the rational West have blocked the red ruin he was unleashing on the world? Many of us, as young men, tried to do so in our own small way, but by then, in 1939, it was far too late.

Hitler did not in the end fool us but why for so long did he apparently delude our parents and grandparents, the Gullible Generation? They should never have been gulled and this much I can prove.

JOHN LAFFIN, *London, 30 March 1995*

A Note on the Photographs

All of the photographs in this book first appeared in *Adolf Hitler*, published in 1936 by Cigaretten-Bildnerdienst of Hamburg (see p. 3). The original captions from *Adolf Hitler* are in italics; the author's comments on the photographs, and their captions, are in normal text.

1

Selling Adolf Hitler

Through his book, *Mein Kampf* ('My Struggle'), and his many speeches, Hitler made his policies and programmes, his beliefs and attitudes absolutely clear. Equally clear, during the 1930s, were the value judgements, on Hitler himself and the Nazis' political theory in general, held by Nazi leaders of the first rank as well as by newspaper editors, academics and some church leaders.

What these men said and wrote was widely disseminated. They were ambitious for power and influence in the Third Reich and they wanted Hitler and his principal lieutenants to notice them. They did not speak behind closed doors but at great rallies. Their writings were not labelled 'Top Secret'; on the contrary they were printed in leaflets, in Nazi Party publications and in the great regional and city newspapers.

I emphasise the very public nature of the pronouncements by important Nazis and their fellow travellers to show that the British, French, American and other embassies in Germany had easy access to the material. Much of it reached the embassies in the mail from Nazi sources because for the Nazis no security issue was involved. Much information was sent to Berlin representatives of the Great Powers by Germans who were worried about Germany's rush towards totalitarianism. The embassies employed people on their own staffs to translate the articles and speeches into their own national language for onward movement to the capitals of Europe. As a matter of practice, in the capitals of Europe a digest of the more significant German utterances was placed

His roads lead Adolf Hitler to his people.

Verging on hysteria, schoolgirls salute and wave and try to attract the Führer's attention when he visits a new road project.

each day on the desk of secretaries of state and their subordinate ministers. Some of the items were labelled *For your urgent consideration*.

We must come to the conclusion that it was impossible for foreign governments to be ignorant about the great popularity of the Nazi heirarchy in general and Adolf Hitler in particular. Hitler was more than respected – he was revered and deified. The German people virtually prostrated themselves before him and they hailed him literally as their saviour. Every day the German masses read and heard what other influential leaders said about the Führer. The Nazi virus could be seen at work during any party rally during the 1930s. The extracts from Nazi speeches and writings during the 1930s included in this book show the extreme nature of the virus.

In 1935 Nazi Party officials began work on a major propaganda book entitled *Adolf Hitler*. It was the brainchild of Dr Josef Goebbels, Hitler's Minister for Propaganda, and it was produced by three skilled professionals, of whom the most important was Heinrich Hoffman, Reich Director for the publication of pictures of the Nazi Party. He was also Hitler's personal photographer. Hitler allowed nobody else to take still photographs of him and throughout his time in power he gave Hoffman his complete trust.

Hoffman was responsible for the selection and treatment of the 200 remarkable photographs that appeared in *Adolf Hitler*, many of which are included in this present book. The book's graphic design was by Carl Ernst Poeschel of Leipzig and the design for the binding and the splendid gold titling was the work of DHW Hadank. We are told that in the book Hitler's co-workers and his oldest brothers-in-arms 'address the public and depict Hitler in his clear feelings and thoughts and show how he has earned the awe of the world and the inexhaustible love of the German nation.' The book was published by Cigaretten-Bildnerdienst of Hamburg and printed in Leipzig. All the photographs, on fine, glossy art paper, were issued separately from the book, in the way of cigarette cards, so that buyers could paste them into their allotted spaces for themselves. This was a shrewd ploy by Goebbels and Hoffman to draw the owner of each book into repeated loving and adulatory caresses of Hitler's image.

As is evident from the Introduction by Herman Goering, President of the Reichstag (the German Parliament), and the Foreword by Goebbels, *Adolf Hitler* was regarded as an important book and the choice of literary Gothic script for the text emphasised its significance. Large numbers of the book were printed in 1936, but by 1945 it was rare to find a copy. I have not found it mentioned by any non-German author of books about Hitler and the Nazis, not even in exhaustive bibliographies. Few great libraries possess a copy of the book, yet it was readily available in Germany in 1936 and had the Intelligence services of Europe been doing their job efficiently every government would have known of it and specialist departments would have translated and studied it.

As was to be expected, all the contributors were Hitler sycophants and their prose is sickeningly bland, but a study of the contents shows, if nothing else, the scope of Hitler's power and influence and his ambitions. Analysis of the dictator's body language is even more revealing.

During the 1920s and 1930s behavioural psychologists had a limited understanding of body language. Nervertheless, most of the more serious students would have comprehended Adolf Hitler's patterns of behaviour. Had anybody in political authority asked such a psychologist to provide a profile of Hitler from a study of his gestures, facial expressions, stances and general behaviour, certain characteristics would have stood out. For instance, the man's fascination with violence, his enjoyment of manipulation, as well as some of the stresses that racked

him. Among these was the deep resentment at the lack of progress in his chosen career before the Great War and the many tensions that afflicted him during that appalling conflict.

My book is not concerned with the theories and intangibles that a behavioural scientist of, say, 1933, might have postulated. I am concerned with what was not only obvious but very public. Hitler was in the public eye at least from 1923 and from that time was increasingly talked about throughout Germany. In London, Paris, Washington, Moscow and many other capitals there was ample material in still photographs and film footage for students to study. The Hoffman photographs were very telling because they carried Hitler's implicit approval and for this reason they remain significant.

In many of the photographs used in *Adolf Hitler*, the Nazi Party leaders' eulogy to their chief, we can read much into his gestures, expressions and actions. From a study of all this, Europe's leaders could have learned much about the man's personality. More than this, Hitler's physical actions, when taken in conjunction with what he actually said, were warnings. This is not a matter of hindsight; precisely what Hitler did in the political realm – the elimination of the Sudetenland – can be ignored. What would have emerged in the early 1930s was the portrait of a very dangerous man.

Among the many aspects of Hitler's behaviour, what emerges from a study of photographs of Hitler is the way in which he hypnotically fixed his eyes on a 'target' subject, as can be seen so clearly in the photos on pages 9, 16 (bottom), 19, 65 and 72.

Those eyes transmitted energy and eagerness and, when necessary, intimacy. Their expression said, 'You are the most interesting person here and I like you.' Hitler linked himself with the person to whom he was speaking in a bond of mutuality – *together we are capable of great things*. He used this tactic broadly, not merely with important people. He made quite ordinary people feel proud that the Führer had singled them out, as can be seen in several photographs in this book. He really had given them his total attention – though usually for only as long as it took to click a camera shutter to record the occasion. It was long enough to inspire devotion from the 'target' towards Hitler.

All the photographs shown in my book were first published in *Adolf Hitler* in 1936. The book was intended for German speakers not only in Germany itself but in the lands which Hitler claimed for Germany.

(Opposite top left)
Days of rest. The Führer with little Helga Goebbels.

Hitler's liking for children seemed to be genuine and those of his propaganda chief were politically acceptable.

(Opposite top right)
'Here, my Führer, is my grandchild.'

This posed photograph and the simple sentiment could have been guaranteed to appeal to Germans. This was Goebbels' style at its most persuasive.

(Opposite bottom)
He is allowed to look through the telescope.

The boy is a visitor to Hitler's home at Berchtesgaden. Hitler himself was a keen user of his telescope.

Hitler never ceased in his efforts to impress his own people and he told them frequently that he was their servant, their voice.

At no time in his rise to power did Hitler and his senior colleagues of the Nazi Party make any secret of their opinions, attitudes and ambitions. They gave free rein to their racism, imperialism, chauvinism and despotism and the sheer hatred they felt for their perceived enemies at home and abroad.

The contributions by Goebbels and Goering, two of the most senior men of the Nazi heirarchy, make interesting reading. Above his facsimile signature, Goering published an extract from his Reichstag speech of 15 September 1935. 'We cannot put our gratitude into words, my Führer. Neither can we document our fidelity and belief in you in words. All the gratitude, love and ardent confidence in you, my Führer, has been beaming towards you from hundreds of thousands of eyes. An entire people, a whole nation, feels strong and happy today because in you not only the leader has risen for this nation but also its redeemer.'

Much of Goebbels' preface is an explanation of his approach to

On the Tempelhof field on 1 May.

With Goering on his left and Rudolf Hess on his right, Hitler watches yet another demonstration of loyalty. There were few occasions when Hess was not in Hitler's company in public. As Hitler's private secretary he was an essential part of his entourage. Like his chief, he rarely wore a hat but here he does so because in such a prominent position he cannot appear to be assuming equality with the Führer and his deputy.

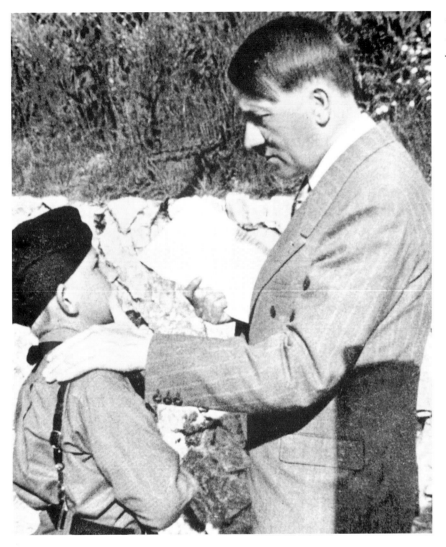

A member of Hitler Jugend gives the Führer a letter from his mother who is ill.

Knowing how the propagandist's mind works, it is difficult to accept the truth of the caption, but Hitler looks suitably concerned.

propaganda, which he justifies in the strongest terms and which he links to the need to demonstrate to the world the importance to humanity of his leader, Adolf Hitler. I regard Goebbels' dissertion as one of the most important statements of the Nazi era if only because it exemplifies his and Hitler's practice of propaganda. Goebbels' own skills together with his post of propaganda chief for the Nazi party have obscured Hitler's own instinct and mastery of propaganda. Few men have understood the art of propaganda as well as Hitler and it was as a propagandist, the *Trommler zur Deutschheit* or 'drummer to Germanism' that Hitler made his primary reputation, rather than as a 'leader of men'.

We can be sure that what Goebbels wrote for the 1936 *Adolf Hitler* was approved by the Führer. Hitler may have made suggestions about improvements to the text.

On the notion of propaganda, (*wrote Goebbels*) there are in the world, and also still in Germany, a lot of misconceptions that are difficult to clear up because they are so firmly rooted and based on prejudice. What is more, in this respect since the end of the war the German nation has received a visual education that cannot be imagined better and more impressively. In this relatively short period propaganda has proved to be a first class political power [*literally, the German word means power, greatness*] for there is no need any longer to prove that imperial Germany was overthrown by the attack of marxist propaganda and that the marxist-democratic (sic!) regime and that the marxist propaganda could only be set aside by the counter propaganda of the National Socialist superior new order.

Propaganda has to be skilful. It is quite useless to attach some good brains to it, according to requirement. As with any great art it needs suitable people to found a school to serve as a model. The widespread error that it has dishonourable and inferior connections must be eradicated. The important thing is the cause to which it is dedicated. [*This is one of countless references by the Nazis to ends justifying any means.*]

The existence and behaviour of great men has an effect on people therefore one has to let them speak unrestrictedly. [*Hitler spoke in torrents and his speeches rarely lasted less than two hours.*] The most important characteristic of particularly successful propaganda is the fact that it does not leave anything out but also that it does not add anything to the essence of the subject that is dealt with. The characteristic features of situations or personalities should be clearly, emphatically and simply selected so that the rank and file can understand them and be warmed and recruited by them. [*Hitler himself subscribed to this dictum of simplicity. According to a contemporary, Weigand von Miltenberg, 'Hitler never really made a political speech in his life, only philosophical ones'.*]

National Socialism and its leaders have brought a natural talent to the propaganda art and they have developed and applied it

She recites her little poem.

The Führer on one of his election campaigns in 1932. That Goebbels would use this photograph in a major publication in 1935 shows the importance that he, Hitler and Hoffman attached to it. The poem the child recited to Hitler would have been in praise of the Nazis, or of Hitler personally or of the new Germany.

in constant and indefatigable work during the closest contact with the people. They have given it the highest refinement. In this respect the Führer himself was their great teacher. It is little known that in the initial stages of the Party for a long time he had no other employment and duty than the one of propaganda leader. Through the ingenious command and handling of this task he gave the Party its true spiritual and intellectual organisation and its political stamp.

By his nature and his character he knew how to talk to his people, whose child he had been and always will be, and how to act for them from his heart. Therefore, from early on the entire love and immense store of confidence of his followers and supporters and later on of the entire German nation has been concentrated on his person. The broad masses saw him from a distance first of all and only as a politician and statesman. His sheer humanity frequently remained in the background.

Today the globe knows him as the creator of the National

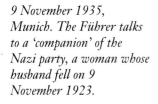

9 November 1935, Munich. The Führer talks to a 'companion' of the Nazi party, a woman whose husband fell on 9 November 1923.

On the anniversary of the 'great putsch' Hitler always asked to see the widows of his fallen comrades. In the background is the Brown House, the headquarters of the Nazi party.

Socialist doctrine and the shaper of the international socialist state, as the pioneer of a new European order and a guide towards peace and the welfare of peoples. [*This was the Nazi technique of the Big Lie in operation for Hitler was already planning war*]. Behind this knowledge there is for innumerable millions of people in the whole world an even more compelling and fascinating human being in the person of Adolf Hitler, even if it is at times unclear.

The great simplicity and the simple greatness that this person radiates not only influence each German but also each foreigner with an unerring aim, effectively and convincingly. The Führer can be well regarded in the whole world as the human being who is most profoundly and most deeply rooted in the feelings and thoughts of our modern time. Nobody else holds the capacity to bestow a new shape upon this time.

In order to understand him fully one has to know him not only as a politician and statesman but also as a man. And this book will show the way. It is testimony of his personality itself, collected with veneration [*the German word also has connotations of respect and adoration*] by collaborators and by his oldest comrades in arms. Here they take the floor and give the public a picture of this great man as has not yet existed with such veracity. They have all known the Führer very closely for many years and they have learnt to admire him anew each day. This is what constitutes the real value of this book.

In it the Führer emerges as the one who has a direct relation to all questions that fill our time. The German nation will readily and gladly seize the opportunity to see the Führer at close range and in so doing personally come closer to him.

The fact that moreover an opportunity is given to acquire this book in a simple and cheap way is particularly gratifying and will contribute to opening a broad access to Hitler for masses of German readers. May it set out on a happy and successful road into the German nation! (*Translation by Anny De Decker*)

Goebbels' propaganda eulogy was couched in the fulsome language customarily used by the Nazi leaders. He wrote the text for five other chapters of the book – Hitler as a Speaker; Hitler as a Statesman; Hitler and Culture; Hitler as a Builder and Under Hitler. The other contributors were Julius Schreck, who wrote on Hitler as a traveller; Otto Dietrich, Hitler and the German people; Wilhelm Bückner, Hitler in private life; Robert Ley, Hitler and the German worker; Albert Speer, Hitler's buildings; Fritz Todt, Hitler's roads; Oberleutnant Foertlch, Hitler and the Army; Baldur von Schirach, Hitler and German Youth; Philipp Bouhler, Hitler and the National Socialist Party.

Selling copies of *Adolf Hitler* rather than giving them away fulfilled another part of the Nazi propaganda technique. Hitler and Goebbels and their professional civil servants knew that Germans rarely valued anything they received for nothing. By paying cash for the book they at once prized it and implicitly they participated in its contents and accepted them – at least this is how the propagandists reasoned. The Nazis chose a cigarette card company to publish the book because it had one of the best distribution networks in the country. The few references which contained any mention of the NSDAP were brief and in small print. People who bought *Adolf Hitler* were buying what looked comfortably like a family photo album. The technique can only be admired.

Adolf Hitler is important as a declaration of support from Hitler's colleagues both verbally and pictorially. Pictorially too it is a clear, bold and unqualified declaration of support by masses of the German people. Heinrich Hoffman may have taken thousands of photographs from which to select the 200 used in the book but no degree of artifice or retouching of the photographs by skilful artists could create the adoration with which the people are shown receiving Hitler in person. In one photograph a young girl is in a state of trancelike ecstasy in the Führer's company (p. 26); another girl, a little older, is vibrant with pride after securing his autograph (p. 13).

As a vastly experienced and always sceptical journalist and author I have seen people rounded up for happy-happy photo sessions with dictators and cunning politicians and I know the many telltale signs in photographs that shout 'Fraud!' Apart from one or two artistically contrived photographs in *Adolf Hitler* the rest, in which the public plays a part, are natural. Hitler hypnotised his people and whatever many of them said after the war to plead that in reality they opposed him and the Nazis, the historic truth is that the masses supported him and admired him.

Gullible, impressionable and worldly ignorant people in Britain,

After the Führer has given her his autograph she is also lucky to be photographed with him.

The girl may have been lucky because of her classic Aryan features, which Hitler admired. Her expression is one of tremulous pride and satisfaction. Hitler's liking for double-breasted suits made them fashionable in Germany in the mid-1930s.

France, the United States and many other countries also admired Hitler and praised him for his achievements. *Adolf Hitler*, a masterpiece of propaganda, shows why this was so. But surely – one poses the question – no political analyst, no scholar of German affairs, no traveller or journalist would have been taken in by it.

From the scant mention of the book in bibliographies and sources, one inference is that it was not noticed by foreign journalists and travellers, and if they did notice it they rapidly passed it over as 'just more propaganda'. Analysts and scholars gave *Adolf Hitler* no greater attention than journalists, possibly because the Gothic script deterred them from attempts to read it. The book was not translated and in any case was not available outside Germany.

Perhaps the foreign professionals stationed in Germany in 1936 – the diplomats and the journalists – were guilty of a degree of negligence for copies of *Adolf Hitler* would have added to the sum of knowledge about the man and his party. For me, lack of knowledge about the book in the 1930s is yet another example of the world ignoring the danger signals that were emanating from Germany in the period 1919–1939, while a bestial state whose leaders had insatiable, perverted and evil appetites was still in the process of gestation.

That so few copies of *Adolf Hitler* are available in the original German is not surprising. With the end of the war and in the dreadful days of disaster and ruin that befell Germany, Hitler and the Nazis were reviled. Few Germans wanted to keep souvenirs of the Nazi period and vast quantities of books, leaflets, photographs, insignia and Nazi apparel were destroyed. Also, possession of Nazi material became either illegal or embarrassing. Suppose a Hitler-type plebiscite had been carried out in Germany in 1946 on this question: 'Were you a member of the Nazi Party at any time between the years 1923 and 1945 or did you have any affiliation with the party?'

What would the result been? A resounding 99.9 per cent *nein*.

Similarly, there would have been a high *nein* response to these questions:

Was any member of your family a member of the Nazi Party?
Did you take part in a rally organised by the Nazis?
Did you own any Nazi insignia, such as a swastika armband?

Travelling widely in Germany in the 1950s, and in a position to talk to Germans of all classes, I met nobody with any information about the Nazis, let alone connection with them. The closer that Germans lived to areas of Nazi atrocities the less they knew about them. Remarkable.

The point I wish to make is not that millions of Germans lied about their Nazi background – of course they did – but that it is understandable why copies of *Adolf Hitler* did not survive. The book was too incriminating to keep. My copy came from a friend, a British civilian interpreter on duty in the country immediately after the war.

He stressed, in 1947, that *Adolf Hitler* was a family photograph album with Adolf as a member of everybody's family. This is why, in the 200 photographs, Adolf is shown with many different people, from the ordinary to the eminent. This is 'our' Adolf made good, a man for all seasons and ubiquitous, omniscient, omnipresent.

In my book I have also drawn from large collections of records of comments, assessments and evaluations by many leading Nazis. All of them add something more to the personality portrait of Adolf Hitler. I have tried to avoid the temptation of hindsight, and there is no reference in my book to any events after September 1939. The bulk of the book deals with the period 1919 to 1936. In direct and countless indirect ways, prominent members of the NDASP – the Nazi Party – displayed warning signals that should have alarmed the European powers and their empires, as well as the United States – even the United States, drugged by the morphia of republicanism and infected by pro-Nazi propaganda.

There were so many warning signs that the Nazis were expansionist, racist and fascist that foreigners could have been stupefied by their frequency. It seemed against all reason that any national leader or party would be so open about planned belligerency and aggression. It would have been a natural reaction for a 'normal' person to say, 'Surely no political party planning the enslavement of entire peoples and intent on gaining *Lebensraum* (living space) by invading its neighbours' lands would admit to these intentions in so many words?'

But Hitler did, repeatedly.

Surely nobody could so flagrantly manipulate public opinion and the political system and get away with it?

Hitler, Goebbels and the Nazis did so, repeatedly.

Perhaps Hitler's threats to repudiate treaties were just so many words?

For Hitler, words were never just words. He repudiated treaties and the conditions of treaties, repeatedly.

Yes, yes, but surely much of what the Nazis said and did was outrageous bluff?

Yes, sometimes, but it was carefully calculated bluff, mostly it worked and Hitler was ready to move when it did so.

Surely no political party in a civilised country of Western Europe could be as bloodily brutal as the Nazis were reported to be.

Yes, it could. The 'Night of the Long Knives', (30 June 1934) when Hitler's SS thugs massacred 1,000 members of the fraternal SA, proved that.

'We were in Germany for the Olympic Games of 1936,' said some Americans, 'and we didn't see any anti-semitism. All that stuff about the Nazis intending to wipe out the Jews of Germany – that was communist propaganda, surely.'

In answer to the first comment, for the duration of the Olympic Games no overt anti-semitism took place because the Nazi heirarchy wanted to avoid bad publicity abroad. And yes, they meant to wipe out the Jews – as well as the blacks, Freemasons, Jehovah's Witnesses, priests of all religious persuasions and all other 'deviants and people of impure blood'. And Communists.

Hitler, Goebbels, Goering and the rest of the Nazis, inadequate to a man, were both pathological and pragmatic liars. They lied so convincingly and so hugely that most statesmen from other countries could not believe that what they were hearing was a lie. Again, that bemused *surely*. Surely nobody could tell lies on such a scale and be serious about them. *But the Nazis were consistently serious.* One of Hitler's biggest lies was constantly to assure the world of peaceful intentions while obviously planning war by building up massively strong armed forces.

In the end, could the Great Powers and their less powerful allies have taken any action to abort the rise of Hitler and the Nazis? I believe that they could have done so but first it is necessary to examine the ample evidence available *at the time* that the German Führer and his fanatical followers represented the greatest danger the world had ever faced.

The album of *Adolf Hitler*, designed for the entire German family, contains appreciations of the Führer from several of his senior associates, and one by a junior army officer. Not surprisingly, there is no word of criticism or even of qualified approval. How could a German of that time criticise the 'universal friend, protector and teacher'? In their entirety the long assessments would interest only serious students but their essence and much of the phraseology is intriguing because it reveals the personality portrait of Hitler that the Nazi opinion-formers wanted all ethnic Germans, not merely those from the German heartland, to have of him. We must assume that Hitler read and

(Opposite above)
Travelling through the Harz Mountains: The Führer enjoys himself.

This carefree pose with an old friend as well as the caption itself shows Goebbels at work. He induced Hitler to appear relaxed in public so that people would warm to him.

(Opposite below)
A neighbour greets the Führer.

The older man's deference is obvious, a fact which pleased the men who selected the photograph for publication. Deference towards the Führer was what they wanted.

*A walk on the
Obersalzburg.*

With Hitler, at left, is his friend and neighbour, Hermann Goering, and
another friend. The villa in the background, the Berghof, was Hitler's home.
Hitler said that he was inspired by the Bavarian Alps and he sought refuge
there when he needed to consider crises. He did not hunt game here but
Goering did. While all traces of Hitler's presence at Berchtesgaden –
Obersalzburg were removed after the war, many Germans visit the place as a
shrine.

approved what his friends said of him, even when they described him as an 'ordinary' man in his earlier years. Little biographical information is given in the album. For instance, readers are not told about Hitler as a son, yet he devotedly nursed his dying mother. Again, Germans are not told about Hitler's struggles as a student, although there is great stress on his interest in young people. Overall, Goebbels and the other contributors to *Adolf Hitler* show him as a paragon of all the German virtues and no noun is used without descriptive adjectives. For instance, Hitler is no mere patriot but an ardent, passionate patriot – and History cannot quarrel with that! It might have been thought that the publicists and propagandists would find Hitler's bachelor and childless state a handicap, but without wife and children he is able to devote more time to his 'great German family'. Germans of the 1930s would have been confident that everything done by Hitler and the Party was for the good of people and nation. They had the evidence of daily experience – they had jobs and homes, society was stable and virtually crime-free, there was a new unity in the land. The means by which these happy-happy conditions had been reached, and the price that would one day have to be paid never came up.

Here are brief summaries of what some of Hitler's close associates wrote about him in 1935–36, especially Goebbels – and Goebbels was Hitler's mouth.

On the day of the re-integration of the Saar, she wants the Führer's hand.

It was 1 January 1935, and older German residents of the Saar were eager to thank the man who had brought the region back into the German domain.

The Führer and Art, by Dr Josef Goebbels:

Hitler is a real fanatic about theatre and opera and he has always liked artists. In his young days he saved his money so that at lunchtime and evenings he could see opera. He writes poetry, just as Frederick [*the Great*] did and he is interested in the philosophers. Long before he took power he told Germany what he could do to help German artists but at that time nobody was listening. Now look at the Konigplatz in Munich, which Hitler built, and the German House of Music.

Hitler as a Builder, by Dr Josef Goebbels:

The Führer sees buildings as an expression of the German people – their stability, strength, dignity and durability. He built homes for the German people and he has built them clean factories. The programme for buildings is to last for a thousand years and Hitler gives his architects, under Speer, and his builders, under Todt, a free hand. The Führer is going to make everything better for the German people, if they have the guts and strength to work for what the Führer wants for them.

The Führer, Professor Gall and Architect Speer inspect the progress of the building of the House of German Art in Munich.

Hitler never tired of playing with architectural models or of inspecting the progress of his visions. Speer was one of the few really intelligent men whom Hitler allowed near him. He became Minister for Armaments and War Production. But he maintained his intellectual independence – the only man close to Hitler to do so. Gall was Hitler's master builder.

The Führer and the German Worker, by Dr Robert Ley:
The German worker in the new German state is now thinking of ruling Europe. Hitler is teaching his new ideas to the nation and the nation is listening. Work is an honour and there is no difference between a manager and a worker. The German worker is upright but Communists and others are taking away their national self respect. [*The Communists were long finished as a political force.*] The German nation is bound to the Führer because he freed them from being slaves. Workers do not need to worry about jobs because the Führer has created an organisation to put them in the right job. The workers once had no paths to follow but now all are marching behind the Führer. He got rid of envy and hate among pure German workers and now the German is the first worker in the world. The Führer was once an ordinary labourer and he knows what it was like to work in all weathers. The workers thank Adolf Hitler from all their hearts and in hundreds of years the rest of the world will be jealous.

The Führer as a Speaker, by Dr Josef Goebbels:
There are two types of speaker. One just speaks, the other speaks from the heart. This is Adolf Hitler. He speaks spontaneously and therefore people understand and trust him. Men think it is magic when Hitler speaks. I heard somebody say, 'Hitler is Columbus! A great discoverer with much knowledge.' He is the first to speak to the German people

Each would like to seize the Führer's hand once.

Benignly enough, an SS guard keeps back the crowd. The expression on the older man's face is one of absolute delight.

about unemployment and jobs and he reached the soul of the German people with that speech.

The Führer's Private Life, by Wilhelm Buckner:
Politics follow the Führer into his private life and he works late into the night about what tomorrow might bring – problems about the military, the upbringing of German youth, German culture, finances. Nevertheless, he finds time for artists, poets and philosophers. At weekends he goes to places to find out what the people think so that he can build the future for them. How the people love him! He is always talking to children and they tell him their secrets. At the breakfast table people tell him their stories about the war. Sometimes on summer evenings the Führer may come upon an ordinary person and invite him to share his dinner with him. [*This is an especially long chapter.*]

The Führer as a Statesman, by Dr Josef Goebbels:
This chapter is flowery with almost frantic praise. Hitler is 'the great statesman', a genius, he creates miracles and is one of the five great statesmen of German history (the other four are not named). The most interesting aspect of this chapter is that nowhere does Goebbels mention Hitler in international affairs. The entire piece deals with his skill in German domestic politics.

Prime Minister Goering with the Führer on the Obersalzburg.

Being neighbours on the mountain, Hitler and Goering often met in this informal way.

Hitler and the People, by Dr Otto Dietrich (Hitler's Press Chief):
Hitler is Germany and Germany is Hitler. Whatever people's rank they admire him and he could travel for days throughout the country, cheered by the crowds. Every ordinary family believes in the Führer and would give their lives for him. Germany has had kings and kaisers but never before has anybody been admired as Hitler is. In Bavaria, East Prussia, Silesia, the Rhineland, they shout, 'I have seen the Führer!' One cold day Hitler asked a man, 'Haven't you a coat?' 'I can't afford a coat, I'm unemployed,' the man said. Hitler took off his travelling coat and put it around the man's shoulders and drove off before he could say thank you. Another man told Hitler that he was badly wounded in war, that he had no job and no money. Hitler turned to an aide and said, 'Make some telephone calls, get this man a job.'

On a trip through East Prussia the Führer visits a farmer's family.

The occasion was arranged to show Hitler's approval of large families. He never ceased urging women to 'have one more child for the Fatherland'. Five members of the farmer's family were in uniform for Hitler.

Under Hitler, by Dr Josef Goebbels:
Sometimes as I am going to bed I have a telephone call from the Führer, who asks me to come and talk about some subject important to him, the

autobahns for instance. He is an expert on everything, including army affairs. What he is doing now he wanted to do in 1919 but he did not then have the power. He was offered the Chancellorship in August 1932 but the time was not right. When there was a wide door to power on 30 January 1933 he went through it but even then he did not have all the power. He was very upset when Hindenburg died because they were close friends. The whole nation sees Hitler as a friend. On one occasion 50 young volunteer workers visited him and he invited the whole group to an evening meal. Then they had to tell him about their lives and their homes. As they were leaving they sang and then they wept with emotion. The whole nation feels safe with Hitler.

Hitler and the Army, by Oberleutnant Foertlch:
(*No senior general could have been asked to write this piece because he would have been accused of currying favour. A junior officer could write a 'frank and honest' account of the Führer and the army.*)
It is a very long article, the essence of which is that Hitler has rebuilt the army in order to make the Fatherland great again. The German forces, says Foertlch, are powerful and they will bring freedom to the German nation. There is a deep bond between the fighting man and the nation, a unity strengthened by the *Hakenkreuze* [the swastika]. Soldiers say, 'The Führer is ours' and they respect him for having been a soldier runner in the middle of hell. When the troops are on parade all eyes are smiling for the men know that they have Hitler to thank for the new Wehrmacht. Germany has not lost its military honour, not even in the last war. Hitler told us [on Party Day 1935] 'You are the new German soldiers of the new German Reich. You all know that you will have to make sacrifices for the nation.'

Hitler and German Youth, by Baldur von Shirach:
Adolf Hitler likes young people and there are walls of young people around him wherever he goes. When foreigners see this they are surprised but this is natural to us. The young generation seems to be ashamed of what happened in the First World War [*the German surrender*]. Hitler is bringing them up to believe in themselves again. Now they are responsible in their behaviour and are working all the time. Reich Youth Day is the biggest youth day of all; the world has never seen anything like it. Hitler's birthday [*20 April 1889*] is important to Hitler

The Führer with the Minister of War of the Reich and the Commander in Chief of the Army in 1935 at the manoeuvres in the Münsterlager training area.

Of course, it is the ex-corporal who is leader here. Hitler despised his generals for what he perceived as their weakness. At left is General (later Generalfeldmarschall) Werner von Blomberg, centre is General (later Generaloberst) Werner von Fritsch. Both these officers had spectacular falls from grace in 1938. Blomberg, a widower, married a 'girl with a past' and scandal brought him down. Fritsch, a middle-aged bachelor, was said by his enemies to be a homosexual. This was untrue but he too lost his job. It is interesting to note in this photograph that while the generals are wearing soft kid boots Hitler wears a soldier's coarse leather jackboots. He had few sartorial vanities.

Again and again we see the Führer surrounded by children in photographs.

On the right is Baldur von Shirach. The romantically minded Shirach, an energetic organiser, was leader of Hitler Jugend. The expression of adoration on the young girl's face speaks to us across the decades. She was Hitler's for life – his life and hers.

Youth and on that day the Führer receives thousands of little presents from girls and boys and the whole nation, postcards, embroidery, travel books. The wounds of the past have healed and the nation can look to the future. The young generation believes in the Führer and the new Reich. Belief in Hitler binds the people together and their worship of Adolf Hitler will never fade. All the youth of the German nation is happy about lifelong service to Hitler and his work and this is the future for a thousand years.

2

Hitler as God: What the Germans Said

All governments heavily engage in what is termed political, diplomatic or open intelligence activities. It is considered perfectly legitimate and it yields enormous dividends for those who practise it efficiently. Throughout the early part of the 20th century the British and French were probably the most competent diplomatic 'spies'.

Much of the work was done in the embassies and consulates, into which poured an endless stream of newspapers, periodicals and specialist publications. All were culled for information that might interest the great departments of state 'back home' as well as the armed forces and the secret intelligence services. All were interested in what was happening in countries that might pose a threat to British (or French) interests abroad.

Close study of professional journals in the target countries often yielded priceless information about their weapons development. Economic and political intelligence was there for the reading in innumerable official reports. Informed opinion mattered a great deal in the 1920 and 1930s, as it does at any time. What journalists, politicians and important people say about their leaders may indicate the early stages of a coup attempt or a level of unrest that poses a threat to national, even international, stability.

After the end of the Great War in 1918 the desk-bound spies were paying particular attention to three main aspects of activities in Germany, the country which had brought ruin to Europe. They were: attempts to breach the disarmament provisions of the Treaty of

The Führer with army officers in the Zeppelin field in Nuremberg. Party Congress 1935.

Photographer Hoffman was trying to emphasise the strength of Hitler's features and the power of his movements.

The foreign military attachés at the party conference in Nuremberg.

This was the 1935 congress and rally. Hitler, and even more so Goebbels, gained a perverse delight in seeing every military attaché in Berlin saluting Hitler. This was the attachés' great opportunity to gain information about German military development but few, if any, went about that job with diligence.

Versailles and compliance or lack of it with war reparations imposed on Germany; the development of new political parties; and the rise of individuals who might one day turn out to be national leaders.

All nations want early warning of such individuals in order to make preparations to 'handle' them. No leader of a stable nation wants to wake up to find that a country with which his own has close relations is now ruled by a maverick about whom he knows nothing.

Masses of interesting information were emerging from Germany in the 1920s and 1930s, extracted from newspaper articles, reports of speeches and books. Much of this open intelligence concerned a new party known as the German Workers' Party, which later changed its name to National Socialist German Workers' Party (NSDAP). There were mentions, too, of Adolf Hitler, first in a trickle and later in a torrent. Alarmingly, much violence was reported from Germany. For some foreign analysts, most disturbing of all were the descriptions of Hitler which likened him to Jesus Christ, 'saviour and redeemer'. But from what would he save and redeem the Germans? According to pro-Hitler commentators, he was the Führer who would deliver Germany from the

grasp of German traitors, from the tentacles of the conspiracy engineered by the Western Powers, from the clutches of marxism and from the vile embrace of Jewish moneylenders.

The comments which I quote in this chapter were all available through the normal channels of open intelligence. Some of them show an unbelievable level of praise for Hitler. Rarely, if ever, in history had such extravagant praise been heaped upon one man There was also an extraordinary trust in the power of the NSDAP to solve Germany's problems.

The comments and appraisals came not only from associates of Hitler and the founders of the NSDAP but from clergymen, academics, editorial writers, generals and others.

Other comments, some of them phrased as warnings were made by authors writing in English. It becomes obvious from a study of what was being said and written that Hitler and the Nazis did not appear suddenly and without warning.

Here is a selection:

Combat has forged the fate-ordained trends of the German community and therefore it determines also their education.
> B Rust, Reich Minister for Education, speech at Neu Strelitz, 15 May 1938; *Völkischer Beobachter*, 17 May 1938.

Hitler is lonely, So is God. Hitler is like God.
> Reichminister Hans Frank. FL Schuman, *Hitler and the Nazi Dictatorship*, London 1936.

Adolf Hitler to thee alone we are bound. In this hour we would renew our solemn vow; in this world we believe in Adolf Hitler alone. We believe that National Socialism is the sole faith to make our People blessed. We believe that there is Lord God in heaven, who has made us, who leads us, who guides us and who visibly blesses us. And we believe that this Lord God has sent us Adolf Hitler, that Germany might be established for all eternity.
> *Schulungsbrief*, April 1937. Bibl. 1, 35, p. 222
> Nathaniel Micklem, *National Socialism and the Roman Catholic Church*, OUP 1939.

The Party congress of 1934. In the stadium with the Youth.

Just ahead of Baldur von Shirach, Hitler reviews rank after rank of Hitler Jugend assembled in the Nuremberg stadium, 'The youngsters of Hitler Jugend would die for me', he boasted. And they did, in their tens of thousands.

He who serves our Führer, Adolf Hitler, serves Germany and he who serves Germany, serves God.

> Baldur von Schirach, speech to Hitler Youth, 25 July 1936.

I am tempted to believe rather in a Germanic God than a Christian one. We are not working for the next world but for this one.

> Dr Josef Goebbels, at a mass meeting, Cologne, 19 May 1939.
> Rolf Tell, *Sound and Führer*, Methuen, London.

All the shame and all the evil we have suffered since Versailles had its origin in our humiliation and rearmament by the Versailles dictate. We must all stand solidly behind Adolf Hitler and show the outer world that his will and demands are identical with those of the whole German nation.

> Baron von Neurath, German Foreign Minister.

Let us show foreign countries which are befogged by a lying international press that Adolf Hitler is no dictator oppressing the German people by force but the true leader of Germany, raised to his position by the confiding trust and devoted love of a whole people.

> Reich Labour leader Konstantin Hierl, Nuremberg Congress 1935.

It is only on one or two exceptional points that Christ and Hitler stand comparison, for Hitler is far too big a man to be compared with one so petty.

> Julius Streicher, one of the most senior Nazis, in a speech at a discussion organised by the German Academy of Education in Munich, 19–26 July 1935, *The Persecution of the Catholic Church in the Third Reich*, Burns Oates, London 1940.

It is with pride that we see that one man is kept above all criticism – the Führer. The reason is that everybody feels and knows he was right and will always be right. The National Socialism of us all is anchored in the uncritical loyalty, in the devotion to the Führer that does not ask for the wherefore in the individual case, in the tacit performance of his commands.

> Rudolf Hess, broadcast speech at Cologne, 25 June 1934. Bibl. 11, 16A, p. 10 *Dokumente der Deutschen Politik*, Jüncher & Dunnhaupt, Berlin 1936.

Blessed are the pure in heart, for they shall see God. The way has been shown to us by the Führer.
>> Dean Eckert, sermon at Tegel, North Berlin, 10 February 1935.
>> Rolf Tell, *Sound and Führer.*

You, my Führer, have given us our daily bread this year also.
>> Dr Josef Goebbels, at the National Festival, 5 May 1935.
>> Rolf Tell, *Sound and Führer.*

Formerly we were in the habit of saying, 'This is right or wrong'; today we must put the question thus: 'What would the Führer say'? The attitude towards the Führer, as well as his own person, are the categorical imperative to which German life must henceforth conform. We are under the great obligation of recognising as a holy work of our Volk's spirit the laws signed by Adolf Hitler's name. Hitler has received his authority from God. Therefore he is the champion, sent by God, of German Right in the world.
>> Hans Frank, Frankfurt-am-Main, 30 October 1935.
>> Aurel Kolnai, *The War Against the West.*

Where a Hitler leads, a Hohenzollern can follow.
>> Prince August Wilhelm, 2 June 1931. FL Schuman, *Hitler and the Nazi Dictatorship*, Hale, London 1936. A son of the Kaiser, Prince August of Prussia was a devoted follower of Hitler.

Hitler is the Alpha and the Omega of our philosophical system, the unshakeable centre of our political thoughts and actions. Every National Socialist home must have a place where the leader is visibly present and where our thoughts can perceive him directly. Generous hands and hearts must, at that place, make him little daily offerings of flowers and vine-branches, as we do before the images of loved ones, in order to show how we love and respect them. This kind of altar need not be in a separate room but in the most frequented rooms, accessible at all hours even to strangers.
>> From an article entitled 'The Domestic Altar of National Socialism,' *Preussische Zeitung*, Köningsberg.
>> The article concerns the personal cult of Hitler.
>> Oswald Spengler, *Jahre der Entscheidung*, Munich 1933.

In National Socialism we see the German Liberation Movement, which we would profess even if it were to be led in the name of the Devil.

Pastor Mattias von Kerstlingerode Bibl. 1, 36, p. 158. quoted in *Germany Puts the Clock Back*, EA Mowrer, Penguin Special, 1933.

Everything comes from Adolf Hitler. His faith is our faith therefore our daily credo is: I believe in Adolf Hitler alone!

Dr Ley, quoted in *Hakenkreuzbanner*, Mannheim, 9 July 1937.

We believe that the Führer is fulfilling a divine mission to German destiny! This belief is beyond challenge.

Rudolf Hess, speech, 20 June 1934. *Reden*, Munich, 1938 p. 25.

How shall I give expression, O my Führer, to what is in our hearts? How shall I find words to express your deeds? Has there ever been a mortal as beloved as you, my Führer? Was there ever belief as strong as the belief in your mission. You were sent us by God for Germany!

Hermann Goering, *Reden und Aufsatze*, Munich, 1938.

On 9 November 1934 in front of the Commander in Chief's Hall. The Führer with his deputy Rudolf Hess and old fighters.

The 'old fighters' were the comrades of the 1923 putsch and they, with Hitler, were making their annual pilgrimage to the scene.

With all our powers we will endeavour to be worthy of the Führer thou,
O Lord, has sent us!

    Rudolf Hess, address to political leaders, Munich, 21 April 1938.

    Rolf Tell, *Sound and Führer*.

We will never approach history impartially but as Germans.

    Die Deutsche Schule, Nazi educational organ, September 1933.

We represent freedom of research but we have stressed that this freedom of research must not be confused with freedom to abuse the greatness of the German past and great Germans from a chair of a German High School, as has unfortunately been the case to an alarming extent during the last fourteen years.

    Alfred Rosenberg, speech in the Kroll Opera House, 22 February 1934. *Dokumente der Deutschen Politik*, 1936.

The angel of German peace holds the olive branch in the left hand so as to have the right hand free to fire when attacked.

    Josef Burckel, Reich Commissioner for the Saar, at a mass meeting in Kaiserslauten, 2 July 1939. Rolf Tell, *Sound and Führer*.

We have a feeling that Germany has been transformed into a great house of God, including all classes, professions and creeds, where the Führer as our mediator stood before the throne of the Almighty.

    Dr Josef Goebbels, in a broadcast, 19 April 1936.

God says, as Hitler does: I do not need your assent for my own sake. I need no support. I am firmly in the saddle. God does not need your assent for His own sake, does he? He never needed it from all eternity. God says, as Hitler does: Give me your Aye. He does not need it, but we are lost without this Aye, just as everybody in the German lands is lost if he does not give Hitler his Aye.

    Johann Lohmann, *Hitlerworte als Gleichisse fur Gottesworte*, Bamberg, 1934, pp. 18,19.

We believe on this earth in Adolf Hitler alone! We believe in National Socialism as the creed which is the sole source of grace! We believe that

Almighty God has sent us Adolf Hitler so that he may rid Germany of the hypocrites and Pharisees.

Dr. Robert Ley, quoted in *Frankfurter Zeitung*, 23 July 1936.

Adolf Hitler, to these alone we are bound. In this hour we would renew our solemn vow: We believe in this world in Adolf Hitler alone. We believe that National Socialism is the sole faith to make our people blessed. We believe that there is a Lord God in heaven who has made us, who leads us, who guides us and who visibly blesses us. And we believe that this Lord God has sent us Adolf Hitler, that Germany should be established for all eternity.

Schulungsbrief, April 1937
Ernst Krieck, *Die Erneurung der Universität*,
Frankfurt-am-Main 1933.

For political women, there is no room in the world of National Socialist ideas. All that this movement has ever said and thought on the subject goes against political women. Woman is relegated to her Nature-ordained family circles and to her business as wife. The German revolution is an event made by and supremely concerned with, the male.

Professor E Huber, *Das ist Nationalsozialismus*,
Stuttgart, 1933, p. 12.

In a certain sense National Socialism is religion, for it does not require its partisans to be convinced of the rightness of its teaching but to believe in it.

Professor Paul Schnabel, Halle University
Mitteldeutsche National Zeitung, 4 July 1935.

The field-grey soldier throwing the last hand grenade, the dying SA man whose last word is a calling on the Führer, are for us presentations of the divine, much more than is the crucified Jew.

Coburger Beobachter, 13 May 1945.

The false idea of objectivity, the old idea of science based on the sovereign right of abstract intellectual activity has gone for ever.

Dr Rust, Reich Minister of Education. Address to scholars gathered to commemorate Heidelberg University's 550th anniversary.

German residents of the Saar demonstrate in August 1934 for its return to Germany.

The Saar plebiscite in January 1935 produced a 90 per cent vote in favour. Hitler announced that once the Saar was again part of Germany he would have no further territorial claims against France. He did not mean what he said.

Good news.

In Germany's government-controlled press almost all news was 'good'. In Hitler's opinion freedom of the press sapped the unity of the nation. He habitually described discussion as corrosive.

Adolf Hitler gave us back our faith. He showed us the true meaning of religion. He came to take us from the faith of our fathers? No, he has come to renew for us the faith of our fathers and to make us new and better things.

> Hans Kerrl, addressing SA leaders, Brunswick, 19 November 1935. Kerrl was Reich Minister for Church Affairs.

Just as Christ made his twelve disciples into a band faithful to the martyr's death whose faith shook the Roman Empire, so now we witness the same spectacle again: Adolf Hitler is the true Holy Ghost.

> *Ibid.*

I repeat what I have already explained before the foreign press; we have done the most important thing for world peace. We have rearmed.

> Hermann Goering, at Freiburg, 10 May 1935.

Look at a marching troop of German youths and realise what God has made them for. They are warriors by nature and their calling is to rule.

> Walter Stapel, Bibl 1, 30, p. 609. *The War Against the West*, London 1938.

The martial will must not go to sleep among our people. We shall never lose sight of our real aim, which is to preserve, at whatever cost, the martial will of the German people.

> Extract from the Steel Helmet publication, *Stahlhelm*, No 36, 8 September 1929.

We must give lead soldiers to our children, that is how we shall be working for the German future.

> General von Seeckt. Quoted from Correspondence de Gèneve, 19 September 1927. Von Seeckt was founder of the Reichswehr.

Chemistry in modern warfare will be chiefly concerned with the production of fighting gas . . . In future a decisive part will be played by the contamination, through 'planes, of front sectors as well as of vital industrial places throughout the whole of the enemy's territory.

> E Banse, *Volkstumliche Wehrkundt*, Berlin, 1935, p. 92.

The next war will require the highest degree of brutality. So the uneducated man will best be able to work the war machines.

> *Deutsche Wehr*, 9 August, 1936.

The air forces will drop large quantities of their bombs over the big cities and the big industrial centres, where sound hits may be expected. Also, as shown by the Spanish Civil War and the world press, in spite of all resolutions and conventions of The Hague, Geneva and Washington, they will employ poison gas too, in an attempt to spread terror among the enemy.

> Karl Justrow, 1928. In his book *Technische Krieg* (Technical War) Berlin 1938.

Foremost among the devices likely to turn the air force into a successful weapon, may very well be the method hardly as yet tried in the Great War, of showering poisonous liquids on advancing and resting troop formations.

> Colonel H Fortsche, 1939. *Kriegkunst Heute and Morgan*, Berlin 1938.

We would concentrate on those three methods which have been tested in Germany and are going to be employed in the next war:

(a) The method of placing bacteria in glass capsules. These capsules will then be dropped from 'planes.
(b) The so-called 'destruction bomb'; in contrast with the glass capsules, this will produce a field of bacteria of the greatest density.
(c) The method of 'drop fields' – providing for showers of liquid poison, more especially of anthrax spores.

Helmut Klotz, 1937. *Der neue deutsche Krieg*, Berlin 1937.

The decision by arms is the supreme law of every war. If we do not succeed there, we Germans will lose every war. Nowhere but in the harder blow can lie our salvation, never in the longer breath . . . It is quite possible that certain cultural circles will indulge in certain considerations such as are fostered by the Red Cross. But that sort of thing must necessarily fail in the face of considerations of final success. It is in the nature of war that everything is made subservient to the final success.

Lieutenant General Horst von Metsch, 1939. *Wehrpolitik*, Berlin 1938.

The Nordic race has the right to rule the world. This right of our race must be for us the star lighting us on the road of foreign policy.

Otto Strasser, *Ministerium order Revolution*, 1930. Strasser was the founder of the Militant Society of the Revolutionary Nationalist Socialists.

The rearmament of Germany also serves the security of all Germans living abroad.

Rudolf Hess, Speech at the Congress of the League of Germans Abroad. *Völkischer Beobachter*, 30 August 1937.

The German people of Poets and Thinkers has become the nation of Poets and Soldiers.

Baldur von Schirach, *Hakenkreuzbanner*, 15 June 1938. Von Schirach was leader of Hitler Youth.

We believe in force. The fact that we have the strongest army is a security against war.

Dr Josef Goebbels, Exhibition Hall, Cologne, 19 May 1939.

Faithful to the Führer's teaching, we must feel far more loyal to the very last fellow-German than to the King of a foreign country . . . The voice of the blood in these people, who for the most part had become citizens of their host nation, must be made to sing forth ever more powerfully, and they must be enlightened beyond doubt that, according to the blood, they belong to us and to nobody else. . . . I have no doubt whatever that the Germans abroad are an instrument . . . on which the Führer is yet going to play a tremendous tune!

KW Hurl, address at the IV Rally of Germans Abroad, Erlingen, 1936 *Frankische Tageszeitung*, 5 September 1936.

The only instrument with which one can conduct foreign policy is alone and exclusively – the sword.

Dr Josef Goebbels, *Der Angriff* 28 May 1931, the organ of the Nazi Party.

To kill the martial spirit and will deliberately and systematically is to act against the divine will. The vague and insincere pacifism which denies its own people, created by God, in favour of the abstract notion of a so-called humanity . . . is so contrary to the divine will. . . .

Döring, former chaplain to the Imperial Court, in *Das andere Deutschland*, 14 February 1931.

Peace is the ideal condition, but it carries with it the risk of stagnation and somnolence; war, on the contrary, is the great stimulant and uplifter, quickening the whole pace of existence and opening up a completely different and, in most cases, novel world of ideas.

E Banse, in his book *Raum und Volk im Weltkriege* (Germany prepare for War!), L Dickson, London, 1934.

Today it is again the warriors who rule. Without armed force there is no viable law. This basic foundation of blood is indispensable in national life and therefore in international law. The German Defence constitution is the pre-requisite for the foundation of a viable order of international law.

Dr Bohnacker, 'Wehrrecht – Eine Voraussetzung von Staats – und Volkerrecht', *Juristische Wochenschrift*, 1935.

Germany's Present.

The caption-writer means that the armed forces were not only Germany's past but the soul of the nation's present being. This photograph is poetic imagery, a glorification of the fighting men of Aryan stock. Hitler himself would have said that these were the classic German soldiers.

To us Right is solely and exclusively that which serves German honour.
Dr Alfred Rosenberg 1931, *Der Mythus des 20 Jahrhunderte*,
Munich 1931. Rosenberg was one of the leading
theorists of National Socialism.

Before the majesty of Life, treaties are just so many scraps of paper –
for the sake of Peace.
Dr Hans K Keller 'Volkerrecht von Morgan',
Zeitschrift fur Volkerrecht, 1933, p. 366.

Right is for National Socialists that which serves the German people.
Dr Wilhelm Frick, Congress of German Lawyers, 10 March 1933.
Bibl. 1, 48, p. 131. Frick took part in the Nazi *Putsch* in 1933 and was
the first National Socialist to become a Minister.

Only nations with the mental and moral qualifications, as expressed in
their discipline and organisation, to hold firmly in their hands the com-
plicated apparatus of a modern community are entitled to form a State
which will be a first-rank subject of international law. The States formed
by other nations can only be *objects* of international law.
Professor Carl Schmitt, lecture at Berlin, 18 March 1939.
Rolf Tell, *Sound and Führer*.

As the sources for interpretation the judges have at their disposal the Party Programme, *Mein Kampf*, and speeches by the Führer.
Justice Rothenberger, *Frankfurter Zeitung*, 4 October 1935.

The basis of interpretation (of the law) is the political philosophy of the National Socialist Party. In face of the Führer's decisions the judge has no right of interpretation.
Reichminister Dr Hans Frank, speech to lawyers, Berlin, 15 January 1936.

The guiding principle must be: 'Justice is what benefits my nation!'
Gauleiter Mutschmann, *Volkischer Beobachter*, 17 January 1936.

Right is what benefits the German people, and wrong is what would be hurtful to it. To establish the limits between right and wrong is the task of the highest party court of justice.
Walther Büch, at a press reception, Munich, 5 February 1936.
Büch was a Storm Troop leader for Southern Bavaria.

. . . Love for the Führer has become a principle of law.
Reichminister Dr Hans Frank, *Völkischer Beobachter*, 30 June 1936.

. . . The Germans have a special mission for all other nations. Their culture is the closest to a universal culture and therefore it must become the culture of mankind.
Walter Pembaur, *Nationalismus and Ethik*, 1935, p. 178.

While in America the greatest emphasis is laid on the idea of *human rights*, in Germany, as the expression of other circumstances, men stress the idea of *human duties*. This is a fundamental distinction in politics and morals. The concept of duty expresses Germany's philosophy and view of life much better than the concept of rights possessed by individuals.

From the concept of human rights, one passes easily and naturally to democracy, while from the concept of human duties one comes without much indiscretion to the Leader-State.
Der Nordwesten (German-Canadian weekly), 31 May 1939.

Europe – the whole world – can go up in flames. We don't care. Germany must live and be free.

> Ernst Röhm. Röhm (1887–1934) was Chief of Staff of the Reich leadership the National Socialist Party; murdered by his Party comrades, 30 June 1934.

The operation of the 'law of space' depends above all on the racial type of the people inhabiting it. There are peoples who allow their life to be determined to a considerable extent by space; there are other peoples, and these include, in particular, the Nordic-German nations, who mould space, who place its forces in their service, who, indeed, feed their own strength out of its resistance. . . . Thus the power of the blood confronts the resistances of the soil.

> Martin Iskraut, 'Die stammhaften Krafte in der deutschen Geschichte', *Nationalsozialistische Schulunsschriften*, Vol. 2, 1939, p. 64.

Perhaps someone will ask: Why don't you reduce your population, instead of demanding more room? Why, on the contrary, is the new Reich taking steps to increase the birthrate! To which we answer: Because we do not understand why one of the most valuable peoples in the world should go under, why a people should go under to whom man owes his greatest cultural benefits and progress, the most glorious contributions to his literature, to music, to the graphic arts!

> Rudolf Hess. 1938. In his book, *Reden*, Munich 1938.

Any student of international affairs given this list of comments in, say, 1936, and asked to distil from them the essence of contemporary German thought would have had to conclude that Germany was a bellicose nation suffering from a feeling of historical injustice; that it had become hostile to traditional religion; that it rejected international law and that it was depending on Adolf Hitler, a godlike creature of unlimited wisdom and power, to make it pre-eminent among nations. It was a terrifying prospect.

The most breathtaking feature of German political opinion as moulded by the Nazis, was the arrogant and absolute racism that permeates so much of the language in this chapter. The Germans were the best, finest and purest of races, the strongest, the wisest. They had a right to more territory, more raw materials and foodstuffs than other

The monument in remembrance of those who fell at the Commander in Chief's hall in Munich on 9 November 1923.

The plaque commemorates the famous episode which began as the Beer Hall putsch. The shooting took place near the Feldherrnhalle (the Commander in Chief's hall). According to several witnesses, 'Hitler was the first to get up and turn back'. More dramatically, Hitler himself said that his rise to power began at this spot.

people because they deserved them. Europe, the whole world, could go up in flames and only the survival of Germany mattered, said Ernst Röhm. How ironic that he became the victim of his own comrades, murdered because he was an embarrassment.

Perhaps the one most sinister statement among the many that should have alarmed the world was that of Josef Goebbels, that the only instrument for the conduct of foreign policy, alone and exclusively, was the sword. He was preaching this, in the name of Hitler and the Nazi Party in 1931. There was still plenty of time for the rational world to react and save itself from the German 'sword', which the Nazis planned to turn into an entire war machine.

3

𝕭arnings from 𝕳itler himself

(I) WORDS

A basic biographical account of Adolf Hitler between the years 1889 and 1922 could be encapsulated in a few hundred words:

Hitler, Adolf: Born 1889 in Brunnau, Austria, to a bourgeois family; in 1907 and again in 1908 he fails to gain entry to Academy of Fine Arts; distraught, he cuts himself off from his family, though he nurses his adored mother in her final illness, and throws himself into his studies, with Vienna as his permanent home. Avoids call up for military service and for three years is a successful freelance commercial artist. Serves in German army during 1914–18 war, performs well and becomes a corporal. He is awarded the Iron Cross 1st Class and is wounded and gassed. Speaks of his trench experiences as 'the greatest and most unforgettable time of my earthly experience'. In June 1919, the army selects Hitler for 'political duties' and sends him to a camp to harangue returning soldiers suspected of revolutionary sympathies. After observing a boring meeting of the small German Workers' Party, Hitler takes exception to views expressed by a member of the audience and makes impassioned outburst. Anton Drexler, founder of the group, invites Hitler to join the group. In October he speaks at the party's first public meeting and becomes aware of his magnetic powers over an audience. Discharged from the army, Hitler embarks on a political life as founder member No 7 of the National Socialist German Workers' Party, the 'Nazis'.

Students of Hitler's life have made far too little of the traumatic effect of frontline warfare on his mind. Despite his failings, however extreme he became, whatever the depth of evil in his soul, the man was a brave soldier, a genuine infantry veteran of an appalling war. He had seen horrors that turned some other soldiers mad and like other veterans of all the races involved in the war he wanted something to come out of the carnage and the waste, something to show that it had not all happened in vain. Hans Frank, Hitler's governor-general of Poland throughout the war, would agree with me about the importance of war to Hitler. 'War was by far the greatest and most decisive element in Hitler's education', he wrote in *Im Angesicht des Galgens*, 'He saw his life as a soldier the only true vocation of men; death at the front was the only worthy deed of sacrifice in the interest of the nation; violent conflict between warring peoples was the highest and ideal form of life for states.'

Thus it went on from year to year, *Hitler wrote in his autobiography, Mein Kampf.* Horror took the place of the romance of fighting. Enthusiasm gradually cooled off and the glorious

At the laying of the foundation stone of the new Reichsbank on 5 May 1934.

Hitler missed no significant occasion to be seen in public. The Reichsbank was important to him because with its construction came a fiscal and banking system.

exuberance was drowned in the agony of death. A time came when each man had to struggle between the urge of self-preservation and the call of duty. By the winter of 1915–16 this struggle was over in myself. My will was at last victorious. In the early days I was able to join in the attack with cheers and laughter. Now I was calm and determined. Thus I went on until the end. Only thus could fate move towards the last test without breaking my nerve or loosening my reason. The objective we fought for, as the war went on, was the noblest and most compelling which is imaginable to man. It was the freedom and independence of our nation, security for future nourishment and the nation's honour.

While my book is not primarily about the reasons for Hitler's dedication to politics in 1919 and about conditions in Germany at the end of the war, it has to be said that observers and statesmen among the Allied victors knew that the country was in a state of primeval chaos. The war had affected the people of Germany in Prussia more profoundly than those of Britain, France, Belgium and Russia, the other nations most directly affected, even though the actual conflict did not touch German soil. The German press had preached a doctrine of hate against the nation's enemies and had foisted upon the people, often at official direction, a cult of brutality, cruelty and blood-lust. In contrast, Allied propaganda against Germany had been relatively benign.

German literature and art were debased, the nation was flooded with pictures of war in all its lethal brutality and everything was heavily impregnated with cruelty and a maniacal horror.

One of the most acutely observant, intelligent and privileged foreign observers actually on the scene of this madness, British Brigadier JH Morgan, noted that the Germany he knew between 1919 and 1923 was 'a savage forest'. He paints a disturbing picture of that forest, swarming with predators and ravaged by passions. The Germans, he says, were more of a ferocious horde than a civilised community. Later I will produce Morgan as an expert witness to the fact that the threat posed by Germany, Hitler and the Nazis was well publicised in the West.

A German author, writing anonymously in 1921, paints an even more revolting picture of Germany in the throes of the revolution that

The Führer visits the victims of Reinsdorf.

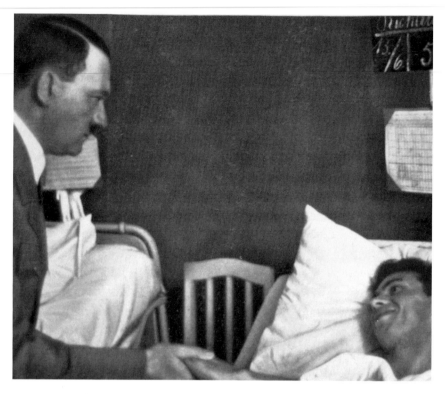

Supporters of Hitler were injured during a riot supposedly incited by Communists, though it is difficult to say with certainty which side caused the trouble. Hitler was quick to visit his people in hospital. This young man's adoration of his Führer could hardly have been faked, though it is possible that the propagandists used an actor. They did so on other occasions.

followed the war.* His desire for anonymity was understandable; had he been identified he would probably have been murdered by Nationalists or army officers:

> The war had been conducted by us without the slightest chivalry, without the slightest nobility and with the most appalling hatred. That is why the moral brutalization which the war produced among us now knows no limits. The instincts of an unlicensed soldiery dominate today the whole of our public life. The

* *Die Trägadie Deutschlands, von einem Deutschen* (Germany's Tragedy, by a German), published in Stuttgart.

hand-grenade is the chosen method of expressing a difference of
opinion, the revolver and the rubber truncheon take the place of
argument, murder has become a recognized instrument of politics,
calumny of the vilest kind is the order of the day in our political
press. Nay, more, in certain of our newspapers one reads open
incitements to the murder of political opponents.

It would be a complete mistake to stigmatize the Revolution as
the cause of this brutalization of our people. That is clear enough
from the fact that its symptoms are most apparent in just those
classes who from the beginning have been the opponents of the
Revolution. But those very classes were the friends of War. That
the craft of war brutalizes there can be no doubt whatsoever. And
it brutalizes the young among us far more than the old, because a
young man is far more susceptible to impressions, he succumbs far
more easily to bad examples, than the man of mature age who has
already got a firm hold on life and vocation. *It simply brutalized the
very soul of the German people*. (Original author's emphasis)

Nowhere was this brutalization more apparent than in matters
of sex. During the war hundreds of thousands of children were
born infected with syphilis. The officers set the example in all this
unbridled licentiousness. Special brothels reserved for officers
flooded every place occupied by the army. This brothel system was
simply nauseating. The utter licentiousness of the army debauched
the whole civil population at home and hundreds of thousands of
German girls were corrupted. In this respect the Revolution could
do nothing to corrupt the people, for they were already corrupted.
It was merely that, once the war was over, the shamelessness of it
became all the more evident. Degenerate German women, in their
hundreds, pestered the black soldiers who had been taken prisoner
during the war and equally the black troops of the French army of
occupation after it. These women were responsible for a 'white
shame', for which they ought to have been whipped. All self-
control and sense of discipline in Germany disappeared. The
German people, steeped in war, became dirty to the very depths
of their souls.

Many of them were aware of their spiritual and mental begriming and
squirmed in discomfort, sometimes violently. For their part, the

Nationalists needed a target for their fury and they found it in the Social Democrats, whom they blamed for the 'defection' that had caused the demoralisation of the troops at the front. For the Nationalists, history had 'gone wrong'. They were exasperated, frustrated and seething with multiple senses of injustice. All those German lives lost and still the nation was *beaten*. It was incomprehensible. Having nobody else to turn against and maim or kill, the Germans turned against one another in an orgy of hate.

It was hate that motivated Hitler, though the targets of his hate varied according to the needs and circumstances of the day. German writer, EJ Gumbel, noted that the secret of his success as an orator in the early 1920s was not that he had any ideas of his own but that he had none at all.

It is obvious from any study that he repeated *ad nauseum* what everybody else was saying in the beer halls. Hitler expressed feelings, he did not invoke reason, and the people, in a supercharged state of emotion, warmed to him.*

The conditions of the Treaty of Versailles imposed by the victorious Allies on the Germans made their trauma many times worse. Individually, in groups and in hundreds of political parties they turned upon one another. Hitler and his colleagues made their target 'the criminals of November', the men who had conducted the surrender. The peace itself did not enrage the German people nearly as much as the defeat which made it possible, for this was a proud militaristic nation that had known nothing of defeat after three successful conflicts. Had the victors conceded that they were not victorious, the Germans may have felt placated, but it would have taken nothing less than this.

As if further to enrage the Germans, the Treaty restricted the Army to 100,000 long-term volunteers and prohibited it from having 'planes or tanks. The German General Staff was outlawed, a blow to the pride of the entire Officer Corps. The Navy was reduced to little more than a token force and forbidden to build submarines or vessels over 10,000 tons.

Remarkable though it seemed to the invaded nations, the German people had no collective sense of guilt about the war. More than this, they had been told that since they had eliminated the monarchy in

* *Verschworer*, p. 178 (1923).

(Far left)
A picture from the election campaign of 1932 in Hessen.

The Nazis swept the board in this election, largely through the votes of elderly Germans such as this man, who met Hitler. He liked Hitler's promises about restoring Germany's international reputation.

(Near left)
Elderly people have confidence in the Führer.

As a group, they had been craving for society's stability and their own security since the dark days of the war and the uncertainties of the Weimar republic. They had confidence that Hitler would bring back traditional values.

favour of a democratic republic, and having agreed to the conditions of surrender, they would receive 'fair and impartial' justice at the peace conference. It was not working out like that.

Only a little less infuriating to the Germans was that the Treaty demanded that they accept responsibility for starting the war and insisted that they turn over to the Allies the Kaiser and nearly 1,000 other 'war criminals'. A further indignity and a financial impossibility was that a first payment of five million marks was to be made between 1919 and 1921, and vast quantities of commodities were to be handed over in lieu of cash reparations – coal, ships, lumber and cattle.

The President of the German National Assembly, Konstantin Fahrenbach was in shock: 'Our enemies have laid before us a treaty which surpasses the fears of our greatest pessimists', he said. The Germans called the Treaty of Versailles 'The Peace of Violence'. After a five hour session of the German National Assembly this warning was issued to the Allies: 'The hardships of this treaty will create a generation in Germany in which the will to break the chains of slavery will be implanted from their earliest childhood'.

With the instinct of the born demagogue, Hitler realised that any ideology that existed had no basis in intellectual reasoning: it was founded on raw emotion, fear and longing. Emotion related to the shame of surrender, fear of predatory enemies and longing for the stability that would bring new stature. Hitler read this mixture of emotions accurately as the hunger for Germany to be revitalised and he gave it focus by playing on anti-semitism, anti-Marxism and anti anything else that would provide the masses with a clear aim for hatred.

The uproar over the Treaty of Versailles and the problems of the provisional government at Weimar gave Hitler and his NSDAP comrades the political conditions they needed. But, with his senior colleagues, he realised that there would be times when appeals to sentiment, to nationalism and even to xenophobia might not be enough. There could still be opposition. In the spring of 1920 Storm Detachments (Sturmabteilungen or SA) were organised. Soon the SA became the most active and the most powerful combat group among the right-wing 'Defence Leagues' that littered Bavaria. That year, one of Hitler's meetings was being spoiled by interrupters until he signalled for his Stormtroopers to savage them. The blood streaming down their faces gave him 'a thrill of joy', he said.*

Vindictive and emotionally perverted, Hitler used the SA in insolent and violent demonstrations and the organisation became the NSDAP's instrument of political terror, its enforcer. The SA attracted political thugs who liked the arrogance of uniform and often enough their threat of violence was enough to achieve the leaders' aims.

Some important parts of the Nazi Party's platform preceded Hitler's own political (and military) manifesto by four years. That the West did not take these intentions seriously as warnings of future German intransigence may perhaps indicate that their diplomatic intelligence did not take the Nazis themselves seriously. These are the major Nazi demands as they were to effect Germany under Hitler:

- All Germans would be brought into a Greater Germany; all ethnic Germans who had been reclassified under the Treaty as Austrians, Frenchmen, Poles and Czechs, would be included.

* *Mein Kampf*, 135 German edition, Munich, 1935, page 567.

Hitler poses for the crowd in the window of his room at the hotel Deutscher Hof in Nuremberg.

His name was displayed below the window.

- All Jews would be denied public office and denied employment in or ownership of the press. (They were also denied citizenship).
- The Versailles Treaty would be renounced.
- The State would hold central power over all Germany; all aspects of life would be controlled by the Nazi centre.

The National Socialist movement which Hitler adapted looked backwards to 'the good old days' of German history, which the mass of Germans in the 1920s saw as almost Utopian. The German Utopia was an extraordinary place, peopled with heroes and victors, ruled over by stern but just patriarchs, often of princely origin; in this authoritarian society all Germans were seen as a master race, an élite.

The Führer cult in Germany, with all its fanaticism and fervour, cannot be explained on the grounds that Hitler had enormous strength of will and extraordinary leadership. Hitler was the manifestation of the expectations of the German people. They desperately and profoundly needed him, and this need increased in intensity as Germany developed power groups of conflicting interests. Society demanded a *Leader*, a Führer to whom appeals could be made and who would make decisions for the people.

Mein Kampf was an opus of decisions. Hitler did not believe in what democracies exalted as white papers or discussion documents. Everything he said and wrote was definitive, a statement of intent and purpose, a positive plan. Some of his statements in *Mein Kampf* are worth looking at afresh if only to examine my contention that the world cannot, in mitigation, plead ignorance as an excuse for inaction in the 1920s and 1930s.

A word of warning about *Mein Kampf*. In its original and unexpurgated German edition it runs to 781 pages; other German editions – there are hundreds of them – contain various deletions and additions. Most English translations are limited to about 300 pages. I have used the English second impression of 1933 as well as the 135th German edition because this seems to contain Hitler's substantive thought. The English-language editions were heavily cut and some of the most controversial Hitlerisms were omitted. This was probably done on the advice of Josef Goebbels, who advised Hitler that certain statements might alarm the British at a time when Hitler hoped for an alliance with Britain. Here are few such possibly alarming views:

- An alliance which is not concluded with a view to war is absurd and worthless (page 749).

   War followed every alliance that Hitler made but not always did the two signatory countries remain allies, eg Hitler made a non-aggression pact with Russia – and then invaded Russia.

- To forge a well-sharpened sword is the object of a people's domestic policy; to see that the forging is done and to seek allies is the object of its foreign policy (Page 689).

   Hitler is saying here that everything Germany did was in preparation for war.

- France is and always will be the deadly enemy of Germany (page 699).

  This was nothing more than a standing declaration of war.

- The question of recuperation of German power is not how we can manufacture arms. Rather it is, how can we create the spirit which renders a people capable of carrying arms. When this spirit dominates a people will-power finds a thousand ways, each of which leads to a weapon (page 65).

  Evidence of an absolute intention to rearm and to mount a policy of aggression.

- It is necessary, then, for better or worse, to resort to war if one wishes seriously to arrive at pacifism. In reality the humanitarian and pacifist idea will perhaps be excellent on that day when the man superior to all others will have conquered and subjugated the world first of all in such a measure that he becomes the sole master of the earth. First, then, the battle, and afterwards – perhaps – pacifism (page 315).

9 November 1935 in King's Square, Munich. The Führer's Bodyguards.

These SS men, chosen for their 'perfect' Aryan features, their uniform height, soldierly skill and intelligence, were an élite group.

This phraseology as an expression of Hitler's desire for world domination could hardly be clearer. The use of the word 'perhaps' is crucially significant. The intellectual perversion of war to achieve 'Pacificism' is pure Goebbels-speak.

The following extracts appeared in the English-language editions:

- Democracy in the West is the forerunner of Marxism and is the feeding ground of that world pestilence. The outward form of Marxism is the parliamentary system, a monstrosity of filth and fire (page 47).
  The confused thinking here should not have blinded readers of the 1920s and 1930s to Hitler's violent dislike of the parliamentary system. Throughout his speeches he vilified the parliamentary system as weak and absurd.

- The world is not for craven-hearted races (page 50).
  This was an exhortation to the Germans to be bold, to achieve the triumphs which Hitler promised them. In addition, since all other races were inferior to the Germans they were also craven.

- Every great action in this world is, in general, the fulfilment of a desire long present in millions of human hearts, of a universal longing (page 204).
  We know from short-term hindsight that Hitler had various 'great actions' in mind but he accurately read the 'universal longing' of his people to restore their reputation, wealth and power and took 'great actions' to fulfil it.

- No sacrifice would have been too great to gain England's alliance. It would have meant renunciation of colonies and importance on the sea and refraining from interferences with British industry by our competition (page 64).
  Hitler genuinely wanted an alliance with Britain and for years thought that the British would reciprocate this wish. As he understood European history, Britain needed Germany as a counterweight to the French. Hitler admired much that was British, especially its propaganda during the war, and he considered Lloyd George to be a brilliant politician.

- The future of a Movement is dependent on the fanaticism, the intolerance even, with which its adherents defend it as the one right course and carry it through in opposition to schemes of similar character (page 139).

  A frank admission of extremism and a declaration that the Nazi Party could not be weakened by any form of coalition. Elsewhere Hitler said that any form of political union weakened the dominant group. He certainly trained his Nazis to be fanatically hostile towards other Nationalist schemes.

- Our German nation, which now lies in a state of collapse, kicked at by everybody, needs the suggestive strength produced by self-confidence. This self-confidence must be cultivated in the younger members of the nation from childhood onwards. Their whole education and training must be directed towards giving them a conviction that they are superior to others. Let no one make a mistake about this: Vast as was the collapse of our nation, equally vast must be the effort one day to end this unhappy condition. Only by an immense output of national willpower, thirst for freedom and passionate devotion can we restore what has been missing in us (page 162).

  Here, Hitler crystallises his plans for the 'Hitler Jugend', the youth movement which provided the apparently inexhaustible reservoir of

The Führer at the Berlin motor car exhibition of 1935.

Hitler's personal interest in, and endorsement of, vehicle production gave Germany the boost it needed to make the country the leading European manufacturer.

ardent young fighters for the armed forces. The Nazi system rapidly suc-
ceeded in imbuing the Hitler Jugend with rampant élitism. And again
there is the awesome threat to take by force what Germany deserves.
Hitler rarely prevaricated; he does not do so here.

- By its very nature an organisation cannot stand unless leaders of high intellect are served by a large mass of men inspired by sentiment (page 183).

  Hitler was careful with his language here for he really means that he and the other superior Nazi intellectuals need an obedient mass, their spirit whipped up by 'sentiment' and propaganda, to do the dirty work. Hitler could not truly be described as an intellectual, but then neither were the Western academics who accepted him on his own terms.

- It is remarkable that the mass of the people – the intermediate class, as I wish to call them – never come into prominence except when the two extreme classes meet in conflict. Then if one of the extremes is victorious the intermediate class at all times readily submit themselves to the victor. If the best men achieve domination the masses will follow them; if the worst come out on the top, the masses will at least make no attempt to resist them, for the intermediate mass will never fight (page 208).

  This is a theory which Hitler put to the test and proved correct: 'The intermediate mass will never fight'. Most of the German populace were of this mass and they allowed themselves to be manipulated. Hitler would have regarded himself and his executive Nazis as the 'best men'. But by his own reasoning even if they had been the 'worst men' they could not have lost in their campaigns to control Germany.

- It is totally wrong to imagine that abundance of theoretic knowledge is necessarily a characteristic proof of the qualities and energy necessary for leadership. A great theorist is seldom a great leader. An agitator is far more likely to possess those qualities – which will be unwelcome news to those whose work on a question is merely scientific. An agitator who is capable of communicating an idea to the masses has to be a psychologist, even though he be but a demagogue. He will always be better as a leader than the retiring theorist who knows nothing about men. For leadership means ability to move

masses of men. The talent for producing ideas has nothing in common with capacity for leadership. But the union of theorist, organizer and leader in one man is the rarest phenomenon on this earth; therein consists greatness (page 232).

The Führer determines his route.

Warmly clad against the winter cold, Hitler made many personal decisions about routes.

> *Hitler as he saw himself – a man of great qualities in a unique combination. He had no time for academic theorists and few of the many men he appointed to positions of immense power had any claim to scholarship, though many were street psychologists. Hitler emphasises his uniqueness. It would be interesting to know the thoughts of British, French, American and other leaders who read this exalted self-assessment. Were any of them disturbed by the hunger for power implicit in it? Didn't any of them say, 'This is the writing of a dangerous man'.*

- No nation on earth holds a square yard of territory by any right derived from heaven. Frontiers are made and altered by human agency alone. The fact that a nation succeeds in acquiring an unfair share of territory is no superior reason for its being respected. It merely proves the strength of the conqueror and the weakness of those who lose it. This strength solely constitutes the right to possess (page 257).

> *Translation: The French, the British and the rest of the Allied gang of 1914–18 had no divine right to empire. However, some of them now have territory made larger by parts of land purloined from Germany. For the moment the conquerors are powerful, the vanquished are weak. But everything will change when Germany is strong again.*

- When the wretched collapse began, [*in November 1918*] and the shameful capitulation took place after the sacrifice of milliards of money and many young Germans – who had been so simple as to trust the promises of the rulers of the Reich – indignation of such betrayal of our unhappy country burst forth in a blaze. In millions of people the conviction shone forth that nothing but a radical purging of the whole system prevailing in Germany would bring salvation (page 269).

> *This passage is thick with bitterness and a sense of injustice. Once again Hitler speaks for the soldiers who have perished and against the political betrayers; once again he calls for a cleansing of the corruption. Hitler, as the writer of the passage and a man becoming prominent in political life, finds common cause with millions of sufferers. This inflammatory passage calls for overthrow of the government.*

Member No 7 of the National Socialist German Workers' Party had come a long way in only a few years, but he had enjoyed fertile ground in which to sow the seeds of Nazism. He was prominent enough in Europe and beyond, after the publication of *Mein Kampf*, to warrant the most intensive analysis of his earlier life, his formative years and his war experiences. His aspirations, his attitudes and his opinions called for close study by experts of several professional interests, including behavioural psychologists. Statesmen in high places should have been saying, 'From where does this man draw his real strength? Is it likely to be transitory? What might he do next? Where are his weaknesses? Who are his closest friends and can he be reached and influenced through them? Can we identify his most implacable enemies? Is Adolf Hitler a threat to the peace of the world and if so can he be stopped? What is the worst case scenario that this man could come to represent?'

'Worst case scenario' was not a phrase in use in the 1920s and 1930s, but it seems appropriate to describe the rise of the Nazis to their pinnacle of power. If only a leader of the democratic West had simply said, 'What makes this hyperactive man tick? Let us put together at once a high-powered team to find out'.

(II) PICTURES

But as I have indicated earlier, Hitler did not only warn us about his intentions and his nature in words, particularly in *Adolf Hitler*, at least for those who had the perspicacity and imagination to read the meaning behind them.

From the pictures in *Adolf Hitler*, reproduced in this book, it is possible to identify his most prominent and frequent gestures, mannerisms and characteristics and to suggest what might be their occult significance. What follows is my attempt to do so.

Hitler buried his left fist in his right palm. Almost literally this is a case of one hand not being allowed to know what the other is doing. More significantly, in Hitler's case the gesture showed that he concealed some of his intentions or that he professed one aim or intention while hiding another that was more important to him. In short, the gesture is duplicitous. Additionally, in the way that Hitler used it the gesture indicated force ready to be unleashed (see photo on p. 64).

He totally enmeshed and entwined one or both hands of certain targets. He does this, for instance, with that of elderly General Litzmann (p. 65). This deeply possessive – and flattering – gesture was often followed by a direct request for a 'favour'.

When standing, Hitler's feet were almost always parallel, close together and pointing directly forwards. This was so whether they were hidden from his audience behind a lectern or whether he was completely in the open, as when he was reviewing a parade or addressing a group of foreign ambassadors. There was no splaying of the feet and rarely a ten-to-two or twelve-fifteen stance. The feet habitually pointing forward in this way indicated a man of single-minded purpose (p. 68).

Preparations of the Party congress 1935. The Führer discusses the plan of the march past.

Hitler, fixing his hypnotic eyes on his official, shows his enthusiasm for the arrangements involving nearly half a million men. Note the position of his hands.

Except on rare occasions, which were significant, he stood flat-footed and immobile. As a soldier Hitler had been trained to do this but he was still standing with feet firmly planted, not moving his position in the slightest, many years after his army service. In body language terms, the stance indicates inflexibility, with a disinclination to compromise. The significant exceptions were when he stamped his right foot, which he did occasionally in anger, though more usually in satisfaction (p. 66 left).

Hitler gripped both sides of a lectern or table until he was ready to lift one hand to make a point with emphasis. This firm, unyielding grasp shows that he was confident of his grip on his subject (though we know he did not necessarily have an intellectual understanding of it). It also illustrates his determination and purpose to the point of obstinacy. Perhaps even more important, this body language had an effect on Hitler's audience. The people recognised the firm control that they witnessed in the lectern grip and they responded favourably to it. Through the symbolism of his obviously tight grasp Hitler was controlling *them* (pp. 55, 66 right, 109).

The thumb was often held apart from the four fingers, which had no space between them. Some behavioural psychologists say that this is a sign of

An old fighter: The Führer congratulates General Litzmann on his birthday in 1934.

The retired officer was popular in the army and Hitler was forging friendships with army chiefs. Note the way in which his hands weave their hold on Litzmann and, by intent, on the army.

(Near left)
Minister Darré greets the Führer on the occasion of the harvest festival.

(Far left)
The Führer opens the Party Congress of Freedom in the historic assembly hall of Nuremberg Town Hall.

Minister Darré greets the Führer on the occasion of the harvest festival. Walther Darré, born in 1895 in Argentina, was an able agronomist. His book *The Peasantry as the Life Source of the Nordic Race* brought him to the attention of Hitler who appointed him as head of the Nazi Party's Agricultural Department. In June 1933 he became Minister of Food and Agriculture and he established a vast organisation with authority over every conceivable branch of agricultural production. Hitler created for Darré the post of Reich Peasant Leader but even peasant leaders were required to wear full Nazi regalia.

Hitler usually spoke extempore but for such an important occasion as this, on 10 September 1935, he followed a prepared script. The chamber was illuminated by candle light, an orchestra played the overture to Handel's Julius Caesar and the mayor presented him with a replica of the Imperial Sword, the original of which had for centuries been the pride of the city. In 1938 Hitler demanded and received the original itself!

insincerity. I am more inclined to see it, in Hitler's case, as indicative of his having an alternative line of approach if baulked on a predetermined one (p. 64).

Hitler's protective gestures. Many photographs used in this book indicate Hitler's paternalism. The Führer's hand caressed or begins to caress a child and sometimes the camera catches the hand as if it might have been held above the child in the traditional paternal or avuncular gesture. Sometimes Hitler's hand rests on the child's shoulder, especially if it is a boy. It is difficult to know how much sincerity to attach to the gesture, common to many politicians, and I always ask myself, 'Would Hitler have done this had the camera not been recording it?' In a very real way, all Germans of whatever age, were Hitler's children, even when he felt angry about their 'thanklessness and ingratitude' for what he was doing for them. His caress and protective pat were indicative of his shepherding them to the new future (pp. 7, 9, 10, 68 and elsewhere).

Hitler held his forearms across his body, often with hands clasped over his genitals or lower abdomen. This is one of the most significant indicators of Hitler's body language. It can be seen when he receives the delegation of Japanese marines. Even when he stood in public with Hindenburg, Hitler adopted this position. It indicates a man with much to hide; it is also defensive and it prevents others from approaching too closely. The genital-protection stance was one of Hitler's most frequently used positions. It is specially noticeable in the photographs which show him addressing mass meetings when he sometimes held his peaked cap protectively over his genitals, which symbolise his driving core, his vitality and vigour. They are vulnerable. Few public speakers, with or without a cap or hat in hand, so 'protected' themselves as Hitler did. Was he apprehensive about the danger of being politically castrated? To know the answer to this question may have helped foreign statesmen to evolve ways of dealing with the dictator. Unfortunately, nobody ever asked, 'Why does Hitler hold a shield in front of his genitals?' (pp. 6, 19, 25, 35, 69, 70, 106).

Hitler opened his face at times of pleasure and satisfaction. Note the Führer speaking on the telephone, also when reading good news. His face is open and profoundly different from his features when he was being intense and serious. In yet another photograph, when he and an old friend share a joke in a relaxed situation, Hitler's face opens. Properly to read his expression in all three situations we need to study a film sequence, showing his features before and after the instant when the still-camera recorded it. A study of Hitler from newsreels shows that in

Children's hands.

Hitler was God and these young girls were engaging in a form of worship.

Party Day of Freedom. The Führer is waiting for the brown columns.

With rising excitement, in September 1935, the people of Nuremberg wait for the front of the parade to appear. With Hitler is the bare-headed Rudolf Hess. Note Hitler's immaculately pressed shirt and the neatly knotted tie. He was much more careful of his uniforms than of his civilian clothing.

The Führer welcomes a delegation of Japanese marines in 1934.

Hitler went out of his way to court the Japanese and his expression here shows genuine welcome. He was counting on Japan to keep the United States busy should Germany have to fight the allied British and French. His personal opinion about the Japanese was that they were an inferior people, on a par with the black races.

public he rarely smiled. He could do this more easily in a one-to-one meeting but most frequently Hoffman's photographs show him smiling when nobody else is in the shot, or apparently so. One possible implication of this is that he was amused by what Hoffman or some other intimate was saying. The point is that Hitler appeared to possess another, softer side; it should have been investigated to see what this man was like when he was not playing a part (pp. 16 top, 39, 71).

The stab finger. As a public speaker Hitler was a stabber on the occasions when he lifted a hand from the lectern. He used his forefinger to open up his listeners, the better to effect penetration of his message. Sometimes the stab gesture was repeated, especially when he was goading or provoking his audience. It was an especially effective gesture when he was attacking some political enemy or 'an enemy of the Reich'. Sometimes he used his finger to make points in discussion while seated at a table, notably when he was agitated or impatient. The most important subconscious effect of the stab was to inflame or goad himself (p. 72).

The lock of hair. Foreign comedians, such as Charlie Chaplin, made great play of Hitler's hank, lock or jib of hair that broke away from the rest and fell across his left forehead. He brushed his hair flat in that way partly to conceal the incipient retreat of his hair from the forehead, a

On the morning of 15 January 1935.

The Führer thanks the Nazi leader of the district of Bürckel on the occasion of the victory of the Saar. Hitler is not feigning his pleasure here, though he may be repeating it for the camera. He has heard that the people of the Saar, having been under French control since 1919, have voted by plebiscite to return their region to Germany – and to Hitler.

loss which is more noticeable on the right side. But that finger of hair was more than mere camouflage, it was a deliberate part of the Hitler image. This can most significantly be seen in the photograph of Hitler sitting moodily on the rock by the lake at Berchtesgaden (frontispiece). Here the spike of hair is worn as an embellishment and symbol. It marks Hitler out as different because no other man in the Nazi hierarchy is distinguished in this way. The hairspike compels attention, which photographer Hoffman understood very well, and this is precisely why the Führer wore it. It shows prominently in many photographs (frontispiece, pp. 55, 126))

Hitler's dress. The Führer dressed conventionally, whether in civilian suit or uniform. His day suits show no signs of having been tailored and they are often baggy. He wore an evening suit with reasonable distinction. But military style uniform was his normal dress. Unlike many dictators, Hitler did not give himself high rank – he was above that affectation. Germany had many generals and some field marshals and Hitler was not in the business of competing with them. He was superior to them. He wore a good quality officer's type cap but again without the 'brass' beloved by the generals. Indeed, he wore no embellishments beyond the leather waist belt and linked shoulder belt, Iron Cross first class, which had been fairly earned, his Nazi Party badge and at times his wound badge.

Reich Party Day 1935. The Führer and Dr Ley and multitudes of workers.

All workers wore uniforms for special occasions, the better to intensify the militarisation of the State. Dr Robert Ley, an alcoholic chemist from Cologne, was Hitler's Labour Minister. He posed as a friend of the workers but on Party Day 1935 he and Hitler were planning to occupy trade union properties, to seize union funds and to 'take into protective custody' all union leaders.

Even in the matter of jackboots, Hitler's normal footwear, he did not compete with the senior officers, who had their boots handmade from the best leather. Hitler wore ordinary officer's leather boots and, also unlike the generals, he did not wear spurs. The image that he wanted was that of 'Adolf Hitler, former front line soldier, brought to power by the people'. For the German people he was all the more impressive because he did *not* assume senior rank – and he knew that. On many occasions he adopted the brown shirt uniform of the original SA but he appears not to have worn the black uniform of the SS with its silver lightning-flash emblems on the collars. The swastika armband – black swastika on white circle on red band – was essential at all times in uniform and mostly in civil dress. Even his civil dress had a uniform appearance: it consisted of black trousers topped by a khaki tunic, white shirt and black tie. Again unlike his generals and admirals, and especially unlike Hermann Goering, Hitler possessed few different outfits.

Foreign diplomats and politicians might have pondered on Hitler's dress – but they didn't. They should have asked themselves *why* he wore what he did, *why* he was so unadorned, *why* he was more plainly attired than a mere foreign military attaché. The answer is that he was selling himself to the German people, from whom he was demanding total and unquestioning loyalty. Why did he need such devotion? Because he planned political and military adventures that would require

Visits to the Reichs Chancellory (Foreign Statesman Gombos).

Hitler and Goering look as if they gave their VIP guest nothing more than the elements of courtesy. Goering designed his own uniforms and was a figure of fun among senior Nazis for his extravagant taste in tailoring and the full cut that he favoured. As Hitler's deputy and, later, his designated successor, Goering attended many major formal occasions.

Visit of Adolf Hitler with Mussolini in Venice in 1934.

The relationship between the two dictators was strained at the time but Hitler soon outmanoeuvred Mussolini over Germany's right to incorporate Austria.

complete surrender of everything personal to the good of the new great Germany, the Third Reich (pp. 48, 68, 74, 114, 141).

I have referred elsewhere in this book to the way Hitler spoke to an audience and to his variations in voice tone, volume and delivery. It should be stressed that the way in which Hitler spoke, moved his body and gestured added up to a theatrical performance. Hitler had a taste for the theatrical and over the years he learnt much by observation and practice. He showed his natural skill during his courtroom performance in 1923, after the abortive putsch. His defence of himself and his comrades impressed everybody who watched and listened to it. From that time he became ever more skilful, until he developed into a consummate professional.

(From left) *The Orator/Adolf Hitler/In front of Hitler Youth/Reich Party Day, 1935.*

The above photographs, all taken at Reich Party Day, 1935, were favourites of Hitler's publicists. Their simple captions were, from left, *The Orator, Adolf Hitler, In front of Hitler Youth, Reich Party Day, 1935.* Hitler's lips are closed in the first photo and its caption is intended to indicate that he is deliberating before speaking. The caption *Adolf Hitler* presents the father figure smiling and gesturing benignly. In the third pose the Führer uses his stab-figure as he issues stern instructions. The fourth photo was chosen to show the clenched fist and pugnacious jaw, a warning to Germany's enemies not to defy this strong-willed man. Taken together the photographs are freeze-frames of raw power in motion and they were powerfully effective.

To say, as some writers have observed, that Hitler would not have moved an audience outside the German-speaking world is irrelevant. He understood his native audience and he performed for them with a finesse and with a degree of success that only one other great politician-actor in the century has achieved – Winston Churchill. Ironically these enemies used much the same body language. Had Churchill been in power in Britain during Hitler's rise he may have called for the analytical study of Hitler that was so urgently needed in the democratic world.

4

Our Man in Germany: Morgan and Hitler

After the war ended in 1918 the victorious Allied nations, reeling from their losses in human life at the hands of the German army, were desperate to make their victory secure.

France, having been invaded four times within a century, was particularly anxious and wanted the Treaty of Versailles to guarantee that Germany could not again menace the peace of Europe.

Marshal Foch, the Allied Commander-in-Chief, demanded substantial guarantees but agreed to renounce them when the United States and Britain, with other nations, promised a special convention to guarantee safety to Western Europe. This convention became the keystone of the 'arch of security'. Under the weak President Wilson, the US then reneged on the proposal and ratification of the convention became impossible.

As Germany schemed to get back on its military feet, the Allied occupation of the Rhineland and the disarmament of Germany were the only barriers against a resurgent Germany.

During the Peace Conference, Marshal Foch had argued forcibly that it was a vain enterprise to attempt effectively to disarm Germany, which was strong from the size of its population, the potential strength of its industry and the fervour of national sentiment. The Peace Conference ignored Foch, who also received a poor hearing when he said that it was

Immediately behind Hitler and to his left is Josef Goebbels, the Nazis' propaganda chief. The Junkers in which Hitler travelled was a familiar sight in Germany. Never before, anywhere in the world, had a politician used aircraft to exploit his propaganda. During two one-week 'national flights' in the election campaign of 1932 Hitler was able to speak in 46 towns. During the 14-day third flight in July 1932, he spoke at 50 urban mass meetings, a tremendous and gruelling performance.

futile to impose upon a militaristic nation an army limited to 100,000 men with the soldiers serving for 12 years. He suggested an army double that number and serving only one year, but he received no backing.

The Allied governments, having virtually ignored Foch's advice, then appointed him to be head of the Inter-Allied Military Committee to oversee the military clauses of the treaty. His first act was to organise the Inter-Allied Military Commission of Control which was to inspect and supervise Germany's armed forces. The Deputy Adjutant General of the Commission was Brigadier JH Morgan. While a lawyer and not a professional soldier, Morgan was such a competent authority on military questions that he was selected to be Vice President of the important Sub-Commission on Effectives. His duty was 'to occupy himself with every question concerning the organisation of the German army'. Speaking German perfectly and partly educated in Germany, Morgan knew the mind, the temperament and the customs of the German people. As a result, he discerned the duplicity behind many of the legislative and administrative documents passing from the German government.

He paid surprise visits to many army units in barracks. On one occasion he noticed that a barracks ceiling was uneven and ordered his men to pull it down. When it crashed down a large cache of illegal arms tumbled down, one of many that he uncovered. His experiences enabled him to draft a 'plan of control' which became the manual for British and French officers serving on the Commission.

As the most senior of the British officers, Morgan had the duty of reporting direct to the War Office on the reorganisation of the German army. The acute clear-sightedness of his reports showed that he had penetrated to the heart of the plotting by the German High Command and the Nazi Party. Bravely, he expounded and defended his judgements, but he found few people in authority who wanted to listen to him. His service to Britain was immense but senior people in the Foreign Office and British army regarded him as an alarmist.

With his devoted staff, Morgan fought an interesting and dangerous duel with the Germans, who resorted to murder in their efforts to prepare the way for the re-emergence of the German army when the 'right moment' arrived.

Morgan discovered that even as early after the war as 1920 more than 7,000 munitions factories were at work in Germany. At Krupps' factory

The Führer in Franken.

The Führer, centre, at the monument for the war dead in the small town of Franken. He rarely missed an opportunity to visit war memorials, even when a photographer was not present.

New Year's Reception of the Diplomatic Corps 1934.

Hitler enjoyed this and every similar occasion because they gave him the opportunity to lord it over the ambassadors of important countries that had mocked him as an 'upstart corporal'. According to foreign diplomats, Hitler handled group occasions with sureness and aplomb but he was less at ease when with one or two distinguished visitors.

in Essen he located a great gun-shop. Known as Shop No 10, it was the most perfectly equipped plant of its kind in the world and fitted with 78 big machines – heavy lathes which planed, milled, rifled and polished heavy guns. Just 11 of these machines were more than adequate to manufacture the heavy guns authorised for the new German navy, but not authorised for the new German army.

Another Morgan discovery was the Deutsche Werke, the new name for the State arsenals. There were 17 of them with historic Spandau at their head. Morgan described them as 'the most belligerent institutions in Germany'. Under the terms of the Versailles Treaty all were to have been ruthlessly and totally closed down, but the German government swore that the plants would be converted to 'the arts of peace' and the Control Commission allowed them to remain.

Morgan observed the development of the NSDAP and of Hitler whom he described as 'a kind of common denominator of the popular mind'. He meant by this that Hitler was a synthesiser – he took the seething emotions that constituted popular feeling, distilled them and injected them back into the German bloodstream as a virus. These are my words, not Morgan's, but he would not dispute my metaphors.

Morgan noticed that Hitler's hate was directed against the German Socialists and the Jews who had 'corrupted' the Socialists, but the French were another Nazi target. In the State elementary schools the teachers suddenly began to teach their pupils to lisp in unison 'France is our enemy', *Frankreich ist unser Feind*. In public places notices appeared overnight offering a reward of 2,000 marks to the first German who would spit in the face of a Frenchman. In restaurants the incitement was slightly varied by an invitation to spit in a Frenchman's plate.

The French ambassador received in the mail a large registered parcel which, when opened in the Chancellory, was found to contain the carcass of a dog in an advanced stage of decomposition. The label bore the inscription, 'The first and last payment of Reparations'. The French repacked the carcass and sent it to the German Foreign Office with a note drawing their attention to an infraction of the hygiene law which the sender, they suggested, had overlooked.

Morgan succeeded in having 60,000 of the NCOs of the old German army demobilised but later he admitted ruefully that in doing so he had 'let loose upon the community the most brutal toughs who ever disgraced a uniform'.

Many of these men joined a notorious Murder Club in Munich, known as Organisation Consul, or one of innumerable other similar groups. They were soon to form the nucleus of Hitler's Stormtrooper units, which consisted to a man of sadistic bullies.

About this period, Morgan wrote:

Between the Nazi regime, with all its abominations, and the German Army there is nothing to choose. The former is the offspring of the latter. The fundamental mistake of the 'Disarmament' articles of the Treaty of Versailles was that they left Germany with an army at all. The attempt of those Articles to enforce the transformation of the Old Army into something different neglected to take account of the fact that a new Army entirely officered, as it was bound to be, by the German Officers' Corps which it was intended to displace would merely preserve the traditions of its predecessor in all their aggressive brutality and thereby only mark time for a military revival.

The German officer was and is always both bestial and

English War veterans with the Führer.

These men might be English but they are not wearing the usual World War I British service medals. Hitler generally welcomed visits.

malicious and the flowering of the Nazis is the efflorescence of this decay. It is a complete delusion to suppose that the German Officers' Corps is, or ever was, a corps of 'perfect, gentle knights' who view with distaste the atrocities practised by the Gestapo. Professional jealousy, not moral distaste, is the true explanation of any antipathy, if such there be. (*Assize of Arms*, Ch VII)

Throughout 1923, Morgan and the other British officers watched as Hitler worked on his slogan of 'Down with the traitors of the Fatherland, down with the November criminals'. In February, four of the armed 'patriotic leagues' of Bavaria joined with the Nazis to form the so called *Arbeitsgemeinschaft der Vaterländischen Kampfverbände* (Working Union of the Fatherland Fighting Leagues) under the political leadership of Hitler. In September an even stronger group was established, the *Deutscher Kampfbund* (German Fighting Union), with Hitler as one of a triumvirate of leaders.

At a great mass meeting in Nuremberg on 2 September, to celebrate the German defeat of France at Sedan in 1870, Hitler managed to stand next to the great wartime leader and hero, General Ludendorff. Politically guileless, Ludendorff was readily malleable in the shrewd hands of Hitler, who planned to use the older man's reputation to build up his own and to induce him to endorse the Nazis' policies. For Hitler, a mere corporal, it was a great triumph to be on terms of equal friendship with a senior general. Brigadier Morgan had access to Ludendorff, who told him that parliamentary democracy was a thing for which the Germans had no use. It is not surprising therefore that Ludendorff was prepared to give public support to Hitler's ideas.

On 8 November, Hitler and his fellow conspirators, including Hess and Goering, staged an ill-planned uprising known to history as the Beer Hall Putsch. He had wanted to begin a National revolution with the support of the police and the army, but they opposed him. Ludendorff tried to rescue the upstart Hitler by suggesting that the two of them would lead a march to the centre of Munich and take it over. Ludendorff was certain that nobody would fire at him, the easily recognised and celebrated general. This march took place the following day and the Nazis tried to talk their way through the police barricade. A shot was fired, possibly by Hitler or more probably by Julius Streicher, and in the ensuring gunfire 16 Nazis and three policemen were killed and many more were wounded, including Goering. Hitler lay face down on the road in abject fear. Ludendorff was the one man who remained

The re-enactment of the historic march of 9 November.

That is, of 9 November 1923. Those men instantly identifiable are Hitler, marching with Goering at his side, and Julius Streicher in full uniform at front.

boldly, proudly upright. He marched right across the Odeonplatz and nobody dared touch him, though later he was arrested. Hitler abandoned his dead and wounded comrades, ran away and found sanctuary with friends. Two days later he was arrested. The treason trial that followed, on 26 February 1924, with Ludendorff, Hitler and eight others in the dock, might have finished the career of many men. For Hitler it was a glittering opportunity. Even before the trial started he had asked his old friend, Franz Guertner, Bavarian Minister of Justice, to see to it that the magistrates were friendly and lenient. Their complaisancy enabled him to dominate the courtroom and in clever calculation he accepted the responsibility for what had happened. But he said there could be no such thing as treason against the traitors of 1918.

With the world's press listening for 24 days, Hitler presented a peroration that might well have been written by a master playwright.

I believe that the hour will come when the masses, who stand today in the street with our swastika banner, will unite with those who fired upon them. When I learnt that it was the Green police [the Bavarian state police] which fired, I was happy that it was not the Reichswehr which had stained the record. The Reichswehr stands as untarnished as before. One day the hour will come when the Reichswehr will stand at our side, officers and men. The army we have formed is growing from day to day. I nourish the proud hope that one day the hour will come when these rough companies will grow to battalions, the battalions to regiments, the regiments to divisions, that the old cockade will be taken from the mud, that the old flags will wave again, that there will be reconciliation at the last great divine judgement which we are prepared to face. For it is not you, gentlemen, who pass judgment upon us. That judgement is spoken by the eternal court of history. What judgement you will hand down I know. But that court will not ask us, 'Did you commit high treason or did you not?' *That* court will judge us, the Quarter-master General of the old army [Ludendorff] his officers and soldiers, as Germans who wanted only the good of their own people and Fatherland, who wanted to fight and die. You may pronounce us guilty a thousand times over but the goddess of the eternal court of history will smile and tear to tatters the brief of the state prosecutor and the sentence of this court. For she acquits us.

(The record of the court proceedings is contained in *Der Hitler Prozeß*, Deutsche Volksverlag, 1924.)

Ludendorff was acquitted, Hitler and the others were sent to Landsberg prison. Here he was given a room of his own with a splendid view over the Lech valley and people arrived with gifts for this patriot and hero. Hitler settled down contentedly, certain that destiny had smiled upon him. He called for his secretary, Rudolf Hess, and began to dictate his book, *Mein Kampf*.

What Hitler had to say in court, the way he said it and the way in which it was received by large portions of the German populace was a significant event in history. It was widely reported all over Europe, but apparently few foreign statesmen understood the dangers implicit in what had happened.

Brigadier Morgan understood what was happening. Proof of this came from the pro-Nazi press, which ferociously vilified him. One newspaper sneered that he was no soldier and therefore did not know what he was talking about when he stated that the Nazis were militaristic. Another stated that he was 'the most inexcusable' of all liars because he *was* an expert and ought to know better. Another Nationalist paper accused him of living a life of idle luxury in Berlin and of reporting fantasies to deceive his superiors into thinking that he was doing his job. Partly because of his frustration at being unable to convince other people, especially his superiors in London, of the dangers ahead, Morgan resigned from the Control Commission at the end of 1923.

Free of the regulations that had forbidden him to speak openly about German rearmament, Morgan went public. On 25 February 1925 he went direct to the German people through a long letter he wrote to the editor of *Die Menschheit*, in Wiesbaden.

I have studied your budget and I can say this: If your army is really as small as your government says it is, then your government is the most extravagant in the world. And if your government is not extravagant then your army is far larger than it ought to be. Your Army, in theory small in stature, projects in reality a gigantic shadow across the map of Germany. That shadow is the old army. Everything that an ingenious brain could devise and a subtle intellect invent, even down to giving the companies of infantry of the new army the numbers and badges of the regiments of the old. At a touch of a button the new army will expand to the full stature of its predecessor. The proofs in my possession are overwhelming.

Your Government tells us repeatedly that our work is done and nothing remains to be found out. They tell us that the Treaty of Versailles has been faithfully executed. How then do they explain the astounding paradox that every time a storm of hidden arms in a factory is revealed to the Commission by a pacifist workman, he is immediately arrested and sentenced to a long period of penal servitude?

'If only the opinion-forming classes of Britain, France, the United States and other nations had formed the habit of reading the *Militärwissenschaftliche Rundschau*, the official organ of the German Ministry of War!' Morgan wrote feelingly. 'Had they done so they might not have so generously – and erroneously – admired Hitler's work. Nor, perhaps would so many of them have advocated appeasement. Writers in the publication repeatedly made it clear that it was rearmament of Germany which had solved the unemployment crisis.'

Die Menschheit's policy was 'the promotion of international peace and goodwill'. It had been published in Berlin but in October 1923 the German government banned it. The editor transferred operations to the Allied-occupied territory of Wiesbaden, from where it was published. Hitler's SA thugs later beat up the staff and put the paper out of business.

In 1935 Morgan visited Germany again and discovered that the great munitions factories were working day and night in triple shifts. On his return to Britain, Morgan was approached by a friend, Lord Lloyd, who asked him to attend a meeting at Chatham House, where Lloyd was to deliver a paper on 'The Need for the Rearmament of Great Britain.'. Morgan gave a speech on rearmament in Germany. It was reported in *International Affairs* (1936, Vol. XV No 1, pp. 74–77) but Morgan found nobody in his Chatham House audience or among his readers who believed what he said. This strange reaction was the result, in part, of the pro-Hitler lobby in the British establishment. Some of these people went to great lengths to discredit Morgan.

Morgan had an extraordinary experience late in 1936 when revisiting the places where he had served on the Inter Allied Control

The Führer inspects the first German U-boats in Kiel in August 1935.

The rapid development of Germany's U-boat fleet was a clear sign of Hitler's plans for conquest.

Commission in 1923. He was invited by 40 members of the Nazis' *Blut-Orden* – the Blood Order – to attend a rally at which Herr Bart, their leader, would give the oration.

From his armchair in the centre of the stage, Morgan found Bart so eloquent that he forgot his own self-conscious discomfort at being present. At times Bart was 'torrentially' eloquent and afterwards in the convivial privacy of the Bierabend at the Hotel Vier Jahrezeiten, Bart asked Morgan if he had understood his speech.

Morgan, a fluent German linguist, said he had.

'Ah!' said Bart. 'But did you understand with your heart as well as your brain?'

Embarrassed, Morgan said, 'Do you mean was I in sympathy with it?'

'No,' said Bart. 'What I mean is, did it appeal to your emotions? Or was it too like a lecture?'

'Not at all,' Morgan said with deliberate equivocation. 'I found it most emotional.' And indeed Bart had almost reduced his audience to tears by comparing the young Hitler to Jesus Christ and himself and his handful of comrades to the fishermen of Galilee who had left all and

followed him. They had been ridiculed by their fellow countrymen –
at least in 1923 – they were dismissed from their jobs and they felt
despised and rejected.

Morgan had never heard or seen Bart perform before, but more and
more he had the curious sense of recognition. The gestures, the rasp-
ing voice, the straining of the vocal chords, the sudden changes from
pianissimo to fortissimo and the crescendo at the end of long and
involved sentences seemed familiar. After a concentrated effort to
remember, Morgan recognised the Hitler style. Bart's speech might
have been delivered by Hitler himself. He even looked curiously like
Hitler, short and stocky, dark and square-headed, the Alpine rather
than the Nordic type, and from Bavaria and the Tyrol.

Morgan told Bart that he strongly reminded him of the Führer and
Bart, consuming tankard after tankard of beer, was deeply flattered.
Conspiratorially, he said, 'There are thousands of just such speakers as
I in Germany. You see, we are *taught* how to do it.'.

Morgan's own later researches showed that Germany had many a
Führer-schule ('Führer school'), but that evening he had other glimpses
of the indoctrination that produced Hitler-like clones, at least by utter-
ance and presentation. Every one of Bart's 40 comrades reported to the
table where Bart and Morgan sat. Whatever was discussed, every one
of them used the same arguments in the same words. Even their replies
to his questions were identical – in talking to one he was talking to all.
'They had been drilled to think as recruits are drilled to form threes on
the barrack square,' Morgan recorded. 'It was mass-thinking and they
seemed to have no reasoning power at all.'

He conceded that, in a sinister sense, they had a sense of humour.
The paid comedian of the evening told a joke which took the form of
questions to which, after a pause, he gave the answers.

'What sort of woman does a German most like to possess? A blonde?
No! A brunette? No! A slender woman? No! A buxom woman? No!'

Amid roars of laughter, he gave the correct answer to his riddle: 'An
Aryan grandmother!'

In Hitler's Germany the discovery of Jewish grandparents could end
a man's career, his comfortable lifestyle, even his life.

All these stories, serious and anecdotal, Morgan duly passed on,
through reports to the War Office, in lectures and articles in specialist
journals, even in the popular press.

His book *The Present State of Germany* (1924) prompted this assessment from the *Times Literary Supplement*: 'These pages should be carefully studied. No one who wishes to understand the European situation should fail to read this book. There can be very few Englishmen so well qualified to speak as to the facts.' And the *New York Times*: 'As vivid a picture of the wracked country as has yet been presented. It is unusual in two other ways: the high qualifications of the diagnostician and his extensive opportunities for observation.'.

Morgan's article 'The Disarmament of Germany and After', in the *Quarterly Review* for October 1924, brought comment from all over Europe. *Die Menschheit*, 9 January 1925: 'General Morgan has rendered not only his own country but the whole world and above all the peace of Europe, an invaluable service by his unsparing exposure of the German preparations for war'. *Neue Zurcher Zeitung*, Zürich, 2 December 1926: 'This acute study of the structure of the Reichswehr by General Morgan raised a storm of protest in Germany two years ago. Today he is completely justified by the revelations in Germany itself of the existence of the "black Reichswehr".'

Despite Morgan's many authoritative warnings and the publicity they received both before and after Hitler's final rise to supreme power in 1933, the world's governments did nothing effectively to counter the resurgence of German power, even when it became obvious that the

On the Day of the Armed Forces, Nuremberg, 1935. The Führer with his commanders in chief. After Hitler, from left, they are Goering, chief of the air force; von Fritsch, army; von Blomberg, Minister of War; Raeder, navy.

beneficiaries of that new power would be Hitler and his Nazis. Morgan fired a final broadside in his campaign to wake up the world, in the form of his two-volume *Assize of Arms – The Disarmament of Germany and her Rearmament 1919–1939*, Methuen & Company, London.

It must have been evident to any calm, professional observer – British and French embassy officials, intelligence agents, attachés of various kinds, for instance – that Hitler was no buffoon orator from a concert hall, no comic figure. Any educated foreigner would have assessed Hitler as a highly professional orator with a wide range of artifice and ingenuity. This began with his deliberately late arrival on stage or at the podium, late enough to engender anticipation but not so late as to make the audience impatient. He began slowly, testing the mood of an audience; he varied the speed and volume of voice delivery; he moved between pianissimo to fortissimo; he used his hands and arms deftly and incisively to underline his authority. He paused for applause, which he then used to rouse himself to greater passion.

Since Hitler rarely spoke for less than two hours at a public meeting, it might be supposed that much variety was needed in a talk, even for an audience hungry for his words. But even superficial analysis of Hitler's speeches show that he had few original ideas. Hitler's talent – and I believe that it was a talent rather than a skill – was his knowledge of what any audience thought and wanted. He gained this knowledge from comments he overheard before a meeting, from chance observations by party officials, from what he gleaned from the press. Even *during* a meeting some interjection could give him a valuable idea or lead him to change his emphasis.

He then told his audience exactly what he judged that they wanted to hear. This did more than satisfy them, it mentally intoxicated them because it had the flattering effect of putting them on a par with the important speaker. Hitler understood the prejudices and biases of the crowd that was gazing at him eager-eyed and he played upon them. As a teenager, observing Hitler on film, I was even more interested in the audience than in Hitler himself. He seemed to know just the right note, the carefully selected word or phrase. He spoke from the guts of his audience and it seems to me that he knew that his role was to take innumerable individual tensions and grievances and transform them into a collective force. In short he was a catalyst. According to several German scholars who have deeply studied Hitler's utterances, he was neither

intellectual nor sophisticated as a speaker, though they do not denigrate his superior level of oratory.

Dining on a one-course meal.

Certainly Hitler's aim in the early years of his rise to power was principally to arouse the emotions of his audience. These people were in an emotive state or they would not have been there in a beer cellar or public hall in the first place. In Hitler's perception, civilisation was a veneer; as a soldier he had seen just how thin. Over and over, he had seen violent emotions break out of men who would have been regarded as calm and stable. The ease with which men could be manipulated at mass meetings both bemused and amused Hitler. Hitler was one of the most politically observant and ruthlessly calculating men of the 20th century, and he knew that emotions could be exploited as a principal means of bringing the Nazi party to great power.

Hitler was supposed to be spending a few days at rest in the mountains though when in the company of Josef Goebbels, on his left, he was always working on propaganda. One of Goebbels' children is on his left. The dish was hotpotch and the party was dining at a State rest house.

He further knew that at German political meetings the level of mental resistance and of criticism was low. He had stated as much in one of the most revealing passages in *Mein Kampf* – that is, in what it reveals of his deep understanding of the German mind.

From his little workshop or big factory, in which the individual feels very small, he steps for the first time into a mass meeting and has thousands and thousands of people of the same opinion around him and he is swept away by three or four thousand others into the mighty effect of suggestive intoxication and enthusiasm. The visible success and agreement of thousands confirm to him the rightness of the new doctrine and for the first time arouse doubt in the truth of his previous conviction. When this happens he himself has succumbed to the magic influence of mass suggestion. The will, the longing and also the power of thousands are accumulated in every individual. The man who enters such a meeting doubting and wavering leaves it inwardly reinforced; he has become a link in the community. (German edition, p. 54.)

For a Third Reich that was intended to last a thousand years there had to be continuum of education, especially in the upper levels of Nazism. Hitler and his colleagues recognised at least one limitation – that of death – but they were determined that their ideology, creed and practice of Nazism should not die out for lack of leaders as inspired as they themselves. To this end, the Nazi hierarchy created three types of schools for educating an élite. They were the Adolf Hitler Schools, the National Political Institutes of Education and the 'Order Castles'. As an interlinked programme, these three institutions had ambitious objectives and, yet again, should have been the subject of intense study by the rest the world.

Hitler Jugend (Hitler Youth) directed the Adolf Hitler schools and put into them the nation's brightest 12-year-olds for a six-year course in training for leadership in the party and in the public services. They were to be the middle level administrators of the future and Hitler's own directives saw to it that the ethos of their training was Spartan. Scores of Adolf Hitler Schools were established and several thousand young men and some young women passed through them to university.

The Political Institutes of Education were largely inspired by Goering, who admired the Prussian military academies of old, with their chauvinism and discipline. According to one official document, the object of training at a Political Institute of Education was to inculcate in its students 'the soldierly spirit, with its attributes of courage, sense of duty and simplicity'. Simplicity actually meant straightforward orders and obedience. The sinister aspect of these places was that they were supervised by the SS, from whose ranks came the headmasters and nearly all the teachers. This meant that the students were indoctrinated with Nazi ideology, in all its extremes, from their day of entrance. In 1933 the Nazis set up the first three Institutes, the number growing to 31 by early 1939. Three of them were for women; most of the women who became notorious for their cruelty in the concentration camps were graduates of these schools.

The highest grade of schools were the *Ordensburgen* or 'Order Castles'. Senior Nazi Party officials tried through influence, authority and bribery to send their children to these establishments because everybody knew that from them would come the second generation of leaders of the Third Reich. In keeping with their conviction that Hitler was the saviour and redeemer of Germany, the Nazi hierarchy went back to the 14th century for an historic parallel and found the Teutonic Knights. Hitler they appointed as the *Ordenmeister* of the 20th century equivalent of the Teutonic Knights, while they were its senior knights.

The Führer during the Party Congress of Freedom reviewing the honorary company of his lifeguards.

The British would call these men bodyguards. With Hitler as he reviews the guard is Chief of the SS, Heinrich Himmler, the chicken farmer turned state terrorist. Himmler wielded immense power in the Hitler State.

The first Teutonic Knights had dedicated themselves to the enslavement of the Slavs in the ancient east of Europe, so there was something strikingly appropriate about the recreation of the Order for the Nazis.

To fulfil entrance requirements into the Nazi Order Castles candidates had to show an 'extreme degree of dedication'. *We* would say they had to be fanatical racists. They had to be 'superlatively ambitious', which meant ruthless, and they had to be super intelligent. This was broadly interpreted, but intimate understanding of Hitler's policies was one requirement. The system was based on four castles, with each student passing successively through the four in six years. The first period was devoted to all aspects of Nazi ideology, but to a Western liberal mind the term 'racial sciences' stands out. In the second castle, the students became superb soldiers – 'every man a commando and paratrooper', according to part of the syllabus.

During the third castle, the military training was more concerned with tactics and strategy, linked to political theory and practice. These young men were *Gauleiters* of the future so they were told how to govern subject peoples. The fourth period or Castle saw the students actually based at Ordensburg in East Prussia, from where the Teutonic Knights themselves operated. Much of the instruction here was philosophical, the Nazis' term for high-level indoctrination. The documents constantly stressed *Lebensraum*, specifying Germany's intention, need and right to occupy Slavic lands.

If it is possible to say anything in mitigation of the Nazi system of education it is that the choice of students in the Adolf Hitler Schools, in the Political Institutes of Education and even in the Order Castles was along democratic lines. Parents' wealth and class in themselves meant nothing, but their Party standing counted for a lot. In order to obtain 'the best' for their children it seems probable that many Germans who would have regarded themselves as independent minded subverted themselves to Nazi practice. This applied especially to the business class.

The tripartite educational system turned out young men and women with minds warped by years of perverted teaching but with bodies superbly moulded. As young officers in the armed forces they were the type who led their men intelligently, bravely and stubbornly – and caused the Allied armies millions of casualties. The Allied propaganda shots of captured German soldiers concentrated on the worst physical and mental types that officers in charge of POW cages could weed out. Any Allied soldier who saw men of an élite regiment as captives knows that they were a credit to their training. At Nuremberg in September 1935 Hitler had told his Hitler Youth audience, 'I want the German boy to be weatherproof, quick as a greyhound, tough as leather, hard as Krupp steel. We must educate a new species of men, lest our people succumb to the degenerative tendencies of the age'.

The Nazi education system certainly gave him that and the product of that system was everywhere to be seen in Germany during the 1930s.

5

The 'Last Election'; the First Führer

Professional foreign observers of the unfolding drama in Germany – the ambassadors and their flocks of attachés – should have been noting and reporting on the types of men whom Hitler was gathering about himself as he built up his power base. The old adage that a man is best judged by the company that he keeps was absolutely true in Hitler's case. They included:

Ernst Röhm, a temperamental homosexual who liked the brutality of soldiering. A powerful bully, he was one of Hitler's earliest post-war friends.

A meeting of the governors of the Reich in the Chancellory of the Reich presided over by the Führer.

Noticeable here is Hess, on Hitler's left, and Julius Streicher, the rabid anti-semite, directly opposite.

Julius Streicher, a pornographer, a paranoid anti-semite and boss of a gang of Nuremberg hooligans. A sycophant, Streicher had neither culture nor compassion.

Dietrich Eckart, a racist and Jew-baiter but an eloquent speaker, greatly influenced the younger Hitler. A friend of Röhm, he shared with him a hatred of democratic values.

Rudolf Hess, dour and dull, followed Hitler with the devotion of a spaniel. He had won a university prize with an essay on the theme 'How must the man be constituted who will lead Germany back to her old heights?'. Official secretary to Hitler.

Alfred Rosenberg, editor from 1923 of the Nazis' early newspaper *Völkischer Beobachter*. Pathologically anti-Semitic and anti-Bolshevist, Rosenberg had been trained as an architect and impressed Hitler.

Christian Weber, a Munich beerhall tough before Hitler elevated him to a kind of spurious 'advisor'. He was one of the killers during the Röhm purge.

Hermann Esser, a rabble rouser of some talent, was an unscrupulous, amoral sponger and political opportunist. Even Hitler spoke of him as a scoundrel, but he had his devious uses.

Heinrich Hoffmann, a sottish Bavarian, was nevertheless a competent photographer and was the one man allowed to photograph Hitler. He was ignorant of the complexities of politics which may be why Hitler tolerated him as a companion.

Max Amann, Hitler's army sergeant-major, had become a businessman and, close to Hitler, he became his publisher. Hitler liked the company of this coarse man.

Ulrich Graf, Hitler's earliest personal bodyguard, was virtually a professional crawler. He boasted about having been trained as a butcher and as a wrestler.

Some of these individuals were displaced by people of a more refined taste and intellectual ability. Powerful and portly Goering was a neighbour at Berchtesgaden, and Hitler saw much of him privately and in Nazi councils. Goebbels, who chased prostitutes, came from the same class as Hitler, was a member of his 'kitchen cabinet' and profoundly influenced Hitler. Over the years, Hitler was involved with several women, notably Henny Hoffmann, Renate Müller, Unity Mitford and Eva Braun but in the early years one of his closest female companions was his niece Geli Raubel, who committed suicide in 1931. Many researchers have stated that Hitler was sexually perverted. Interestingly, foreign governments seem to have had very little information about Hitler's sexual proclivities in the 1920s and 1930s, which further suggests that he was not being adequately studied. A lengthy chart would be necessary to plot movements into and out of Hitler's interlinked political, army and private circles.

After the abortive 1923 putsch, Hitler had been banned from public speaking for two years, an indirect compliment to the power of his oratory, but when he was released from prison he quickly re-established a new party. His insufferable arrogance alienated many people but attracted other misfits who saw in Hitler an opportunity to be arrogant in his name. He found reasons for breaking with Ludendorff, who had shamed him during the Beer Hall Putsch by bravely standing his ground when everybody else was lying down or running away. In April 1925 Hitler even dropped Röhm over the organisation of the SA. To resolve various problems he called a conference of senior leaders at Bamberg in February 1926 and presented his demands in a five-hour speech. Perhaps this *tour de force* tired out his opponents and was responsible for the total victory that Hitler achieved. At this time he became close to Josef Goebbels, whom he appointed *Gauleiter* (regional party leader) of Berlin.

Methodically he went about increasing his power by creating innumerable new departments at party headquarters, such as those responsible for women, youth, students, teachers, doctors, journalists, culture and education. Since he himself appointed each departmental head, these men owed their status and careers to Hitler and in every sense were his creatures. He even incited disputes and divisions among them in order to force the protagonists to appeal to him for arbitration and decision, another ruse to increase his power. In parliamentary terms

Nazi power was slender. In 1924 the NSDAP had gained 907,300 votes, but in 1928 the number fell to 811,000 votes and 12 seats in the Reichstag.

Hitler needed support from the great German middle class and this he gained through complex political horsetrading in 1928 and 1929, when party membership rose from 120,000 to 178,000. For the first time, industrialists began to contribute to Nazi Party funds and by 1930 the Nazis were a major factor in German politics. As German parliamentary democracy gradually broke down Hitler faced a serious problem. The SA, under Ernst Röhm's leadership, was now nothing less than a private army and, with 500,000 men, it was powerful. The whole country was plagued by street brawls between the SA 'Brownshirts' and the supposed 'Marxists'.

Hitler's problem was this: he favoured violence in order to intimidate opponents and he encouraged the growing grandeur of Nazi rallies to awe ordinary people, but he could not approve a putsch by the SA. The Army High Command would never back such an extreme action and Hitler wanted above all to maintain good relations with the army.

Many of the SA thugs, even while striding to power in company with Hitler, considered him to be nothing more than a hesitant petty bourgeois, afraid to get blood on his hands. But he encouraged *them* in their blood-letting. On 22 August 1932 five members of the SA were condemned to death for the savage murder of a Communist worker in Upper Silesia. This sentencing followed a government emergency decree on 9 August against political terror. On the day that the sentence was announced Hitler sent an open telegram to the SA killers expressing his 'unbounded admiration' for them. This was outright public support for political terror. Hitler was not making an error of judgement, because he knew that the great majority of the middle classes – his 'intermediate class' – secretly applauded the murder of Communists. Nazi propaganda against the Communists had been effective. In 1933, with Hitler in power, the SA murderers were pardoned.

Despite SA backing, even with Goebbels' formidable propaganda, Hitler might still have dropped into the overflowing dustbin of failed German politicians except for a change in the balance of power in the period 1930–33.

Presidential style government was taking over from parliamentary democracy, and successive chancellors were urging President

Hitler and his Chief of Staff, Lutze, in the Reich Chancellory.

Viktor Lutze was able enough, but was so colourless that he did not loom large in the Nazi hierarchy. At one time he was head of the SA. In the background is a portrait of Frederick the Great, whom Hitler admired.

Hindenburg to employ 'emergency powers' as the only way they could get legislation into effect. Chancellor Heinrich Brüning went so far as to ask party leaders to back him in extending the ancient President Hindenburg's term of office without an election campaign. Hitler objected but in the subsequent election Hindenburg emerged with a clear lead, though not the absolute majority necessary. Hitler gained 11.3 million votes, and in the second round 13.7 million, but Hindenburg secured 19.3 million.

Hitler was frenetically active, fighting five major election campaigns

With the D-2600 over Nuremberg. Hitler had a personal plane from 1935 but before that year he used a specially hired Lufthansa aircraft. The ancient city of Nuremberg saw more Nazi spectacles than any other city, with the possible exception of Munich. Most of what can be seen in this photograph was reduced to rubble by Allied bombing.

in the period March–November 1932. In April Chancellor Brüning banned the SA and the SS, as a threat to public order. This was a sharp embarrassment to Hitler but he covered it well by endorsing the legality of the order.

In an attempt to overcome general unrest in Germany the government dissolved the Reichstag, and called fresh elections, a step that made the Nazi leadership almost deliriously happy. Hitler's confidence that he would do well was amply justified. With 230 seats in the Reichstag and 13.7 million votes, the Nazis were the largest party. In coalition talks with the Catholic Centre Party, Hitler adopted his bullying style and insisted on the chancellorship for himself and sought an enabling bill to rule by decree, making a parliamentary majority unnecessary. This high-handed dictatorial step should have sounded alarm bells throughout Europe. When the terms were rejected, Hitler became angry and threatened to unleash his Brownshirts in violent demonstrations. For people who prized peace this crude and potentially violent blackmail was even more alarming, but over and over again Hitler showed that he was ready to use naked force to achieve his ends.

Hindenburg was feeble but not without spirit, and calling Hitler to the presidential palace he talked down the vociferous Hitler and said that he would go no further than to include some Nazis in a coalition cabinet. Hitler stormed out and, blinded by the red mist of power hunger, he held to his extreme position for 16 weeks. He is said to have told a colleague: 'I have no time to wait. I must have power soon in order to solve the colossal tasks in the time remaining to me. I must! I must!' He may have been referring to his fear that he had colonic cancer, a groundless anxiety. In August, as tension mounted, an American correspondent asked him if he would march on Berlin with the SA and SS 'Why should I march on Berlin?' Hitler said. 'I am there already. Your question should be, Who is going to march out of Berlin?'

Nevertheless, marching to war was on Hitler's mind in 1932. The Nazi Party had taken to its heart Professor Ewald Banse, who that year published his book *Wehrwissenschaft* (The Science of Military Defence), Leipzig, 1932. The Nazis based their doctrine on war on this book, and to show their admiration for Banse they used their influence to have him installed in the chair of military science at Brunswick University. Banse was no great military thinker but the Nazis' approval of his work led to *Wehrwissenschaft* being accepted by all professors of military science at German universities and even by the army, at least in its philosophical terms.

War, said Banse, was determined first of all by moral factors while material factors were only secondary. The concept of war must get away from the idea of chivalrous combat and use food blockades and 'campaigns of lies destined to ruin the enemy's prestige'. Birthrates had to be accelerated to supply effectives and military science must 'seek to create a general desire for war and victory'. Banse was enthusiastic and perversely lyrical in presenting his philosophy of war.

War is not only a factor of extermination but a principle of regeneration. It alone enables the human soul to reveal all its riches and all its force. Biology will stamp the next war as an extermination fight of entire nations. . . . Methods to be considered are infection of drinking water and other water with typhoid bacillus; also the introduction of typhoid fever through fleas and of plague through artificially infected rats. By landing in the back regions of enemy countries and discharging carriers of disease, airplanes especially should achieve very favourable results.

It is ridiculous to attempt to liberate ourselves from the chains of Versailles unless we take our destiny in our hands and unless we work at our moral preparation and at our science of war. For there can be no doubt for anyone – between our present misery and our future happiness, there is war. This is why everybody, man, woman and child must know what war is.

The Nazi party newspaper noted 'Our movement, whose tendencies harmonise with those of the professor, has given him academic justice by awarding him a professorial chair'.

Before Banse's theories could be put into practice Hitler had internal political battles and conspiracies to preoccupy him, and all the time he spoke in terms of conflict. One of his utterances at this time, in early 1933, came straight off the Western Front battlefield of the Great War. 'The more events move to their climax the more sacrifices are called for in the battle' he said. 'The battle will be decided by the man who leads the last battalion onto the battlefield'.

This phraseology is interesting because it could have been framed by any one of the many senior British, French or German military butchers who believed that to win they had only to inflict more casualties on the enemy than they themselves suffered. At another time Hitler described himself as 'a man of violence' and 'the hardest man in Germany'. Studied analytically at the time – *had* they been studied – Hitler's words were alarming.

The infighting at this time was extraordinarily bitter and complex with the Nazi leadership split into vituperative factions. Many people believed that the impatient, inflexible Hitler was destroying himself and the party – some hoped that he was.

The powerful, influential and conniving Franz von Papen, a former chancellor, took a hand in a conspiracy, also involving Oskar von

On his journeys through Germany the Führer prefers an open car.

This was true, because Hitler wanted to be recognised and when this happened he generally ordered his chauffeur to stop so that he could greet the people.

Hindenburg, the president's son, Meissner, the president's secretary and Hitler himself to appoint Hitler as Vice Chancellor. Hindenburg, struggling against senility, nevertheless knew what was happening. He sensed that Hitler would use the legitimacy of the political system to gain power step by step and then rule as dictator. Nominally he became vice chancellor following the meeting with Hindenburg on 19 November 1932 but it was a meaningless title and post for the man whom Hindenburg still referred to in private as 'the Austrian corporal'. In fact, Hitler had been a German since 25 February 1932. He gained German citizenship through a farcical and cynical manoeuvre that showed the Nazis would go to any lengths to legitimise Hitler. The Minister of the Interior of the State of Brunswick was a Nazi and he was induced to name Hitler as an attaché of the Legation of Brunswick in Berlin. Legally, Hitler automatically became a citizen of Brunswick and hence of Germany. He was thus eligible to run as president of Germany.

The pressures on the ailing Hindenburg mounted and he was quite incapable of comprehending the complexities of the political situation. At noon on 30 January 1933, a bleak and snowy day in Berlin, the president signed the document that appointed Hitler to be Chancellor. It was a perfectly constitutional step, even though many Germans did not understand that what had happened was a monumental tragedy. William Shirer expresses the situation in a sublimely succinct sentence: 'The Germans imposed the Nazi tyranny on themselves'. (In his seminal *The Rise and Fall of the Third Reich*, Secker & Warburg, 1959, page 187).

On 20 February 1933 Chancellor Hitler addressed a meeting of major industrialists to appeal for funds for the Nazi Party. He offered them a good deal for their money – basically, law and order. Further, to win the support of the tycoons he promised that the next campaign at the polls would be 'the last election'. And he meant it – though not in the way his audience understood. They were sick and tired of the all too frequent electioneering instability. Hitler was fed up with the exasperations of democracy itself, which he called a 'monstrosity of filth and fire'.

On the night of 27 February 1933 a great and dramatic event occurred. The splendid buildings of the Reichstag, the German parliament, went up in flames. This event, which shocked the nation, was allegedly the work of a feeble-minded former Dutch communist, Marinus van der Lubbe, and it gave the Nazis a political gift of tremendous proportions. They had planned a positive but slow and steady campaign to eradicate their political opponents, but the Reichstag fire gave them the opportunity to claim that it was the signal for a general Communist uprising. In Goebbels' masterly hands 'a conspiracy was about to destroy Germany'. Amid a welter of arrests, restrictions and prohibitions came the presidential state of emergency 'to save the state from Communists acts of violence'. The decree was signed by Hindenburg but framed by Hitler. The Gestapo, the SS and the SA began the reign of terror for which they had long been preparing.

All enemies of the Nazis became victims of the terror, not merely the

President of the Reich von Hindenburg and Chancellor of the Reich Hitler.

The last photograph of the two men together. Hindenburg was 94 and from the moment of his death the Nazi Party banned publication of his photograph.

Communists. It was not in the least strange to Brigadier JH Morgan and other foreigners who understood the Nazis' plot for all the German democratic parties to dissolve themselves within a few weeks of Hitler's rise to power. They did this not as a protest, but as an amazing demonstration of confidence in Hitler and the Nazis. Overwhelmingly they consisted of the middle classes and they welcomed Hitler and his gang as the party of law, order and stability. Almost to a man and woman these people would later protest that they were not Nazis, nevertheless they surrendered to them with craven rapidity. And they knew that the Nazi Party was led by perverts, psychopaths, sadists, anti-semites, bullies, eccentrics and misfits generally.

There were some brave and honourable exceptions who kept to their principles and fought on. When Hindenburg appointed Hitler to be Chancellor on 30 January, an alarmed democratic professor had issued a pamphlet warning of the encroaching dangers of dictatorship. After the Reichstag fire he printed another leaflet expressing the opinion – shared by many – that the Nazis themselves had started the fire in order to mount a wave of terror on which they could ride to total power.

Next he tried to form a league to fight 'the Law of 7 April' because he discerned that it meant handing over government to Nazi control. Bravely, and still alone, he issued a pamphlet warning Catholics that the Concordat signed between Hitler and the Vatican on 8 July would be repudiated by Hitler as soon as he had exploited the Catholics to the limit.

On 13 July in a Reichstag speech, Hitler announced, 'Everyone must know for all future time that if he raises his hand or voice to strike at the State then certain death is his lot'. Just three days later the NSDAP was declared the only legal party.

On that day, 16 July, the courageous professor, still fighting for democracy, went out for his daily walk and did not return. A few months later his wife received a cigar box marked with a swastika and the word 'traitor' before her husband's name. The box contained his ashes. The Nazis dealt with many lone enemies in this way.

One of the many foreign journalists in Germany during Hitler's spring and summer of satisfaction, 1933, was the American Leland Stowe, who reported that Hitler and his Nazis had firmly decided on war, not merely war for liberation but for 'expansion and glorification'. (*Nazi Germany Means War*, Faber & Faber, 1933.) Stowe visited the Great War museum in Unter den Linden, one of Berlin's great thoroughfares, and found a section of front-line trench recreated with stark realism and great skill – 'scenes of mud, blood and corpses'. Most of the people assembling there, he noted from their uniforms and swastika brassards, were Nazis of all ages and 'they came away with a strange, hungry light in their eyes'.

On 9 May, with the Nazi government in power for only two months, Stowe reported that Reichminister Frick had announced a new law for German schools. 'The military idea', said Frick, 'must find ample treatment in school instruction. The German people must learn once more . . .'

Stowe spent weeks visiting German schools to see how the germ was planted:

> The children do a great deal of marching. They march in and they march out; often they march at recess-time. Frequently they are marched for blocks through city or town before they are allowed to disband. Soon they get to the point where they would rather march anyway. They sing patriotic songs and give salutes; a child feels important and grown-up doing this. The Hitler Jugend have many excellent martial tunes and they now have the theme song of the great child's propaganda film, *Hitler Junger Quex*. You must hear shrill childish voices singing a song like this to appreciate what the Nazi movement is doing to the spirit of German youth.
>
> > Unsere Fahne ist die neue Zeit,
> > Und die Fahne führt uns in die Ewigkeit.
> > Ja, die Fahne ist mehr als der Tod.
> > (Our flag is the new era
> > And the flag leads us to Eternity.
> > Yes, the flag is more than death.)

On 31 October 1933 Stowe witnessed a chilling parade of several hundred Hitler Jugend in Westphalia. A monument to the Archangel Michael was to be unveiled and a Hitler Jugend leader addressed the boys: 'The ancient march-order, which is protected by our fallen heroes, reads, "Our decision is for bloody sacrificing". This archangel is leading the front of comrades, a front formed by warriors of the Reich who have only one enemy – the opponents of the Reich and its rulership. We do not want to speak the warm words of peace here. Our words are dictated by the terrible appeal of war. Young crew, raise the hand of oath before the monument, which is dedicated to the sublimity of blood-letting'.

Stowe pointed out that the German character was not suited for conscientious objectors and that Hitler Jugend boys were systematically beating up classmates who did not join the movement.

9 November 1934 in Munich. In front of the Hall of the Commander in Chief the Führer addresses newly enrolled members of Hitler Jugend and the League of German Maidens.

Here we see Hitler's grip on the lectern.

You cannot preach force to youngsters without being taken at your word. Germany's youth are millions strong. They are being channelled, thoroughly and passionately, in one direction. That direction is not the one which Adolf Hitler seemed to indicate when he said, 'Germany wants nothing but peace'. Can any nation's rulers teach war and get peace? (Stowe, *ibid.*)

Stowe was only one of numerous foreign correspondents who were concerned and alarmed about Chancellor Hitler's policy of war, but their warnings were ignored.

In October 1933 Chancellor Hitler withdrew the German Reich from the League of Nations, a radical step that shouted aloud his foreign policy intentions. He would not be bound by the League's treaties, votes or motions – Germany would be a law unto itself. He stated, as if in so many words, that neither Germany as a nation nor Hitler as a leader felt any obligation to international law and would not be influenced by appeals, adjurations or exhortations from abroad. It was a declaration of separation from the rest of the world.

No decision that Hitler made, before actually going to war, was as far-reaching as his withdrawal from the League of Nations. Its significance could not possibly have been lost on the world's statesmen, and, indeed, foreign governments opposed the German move. Hitler, in consultation with his inner circle, decided that the German people would support him and thus snub the world. He announced that a plebiscite would take place, coupled with elections for a new all-Nazi Reichstag.

The government instructed the various provincial and county governments to send telegrams to Berlin. In effect, they all said the same: 'The population of (region or city) approves the Reich government's actions and calls for peace, bread and work'.

The plebiscite campaign which then took place was a model in its organisational thoroughness and an example of Nazi methods. The Nazis went to enormous trouble even though the overall vote was beyond question since the NSDAP would alone count the ballots. The exercise was to 'prove' that electioneering was honest and open and that voting would be free – even though people were now compelled to attend Nazi meetings. Despite the compulsion, fares on trains and buses were nominal and bands were provided for the people's entertainment.

All this was advanced as 'evidence' that people attended meetings by choice.

The serious business of electioneering commenced 10 days before the poll. First came a great parade which culminated in a rally with the usual swathes of flags. Every building and private house also wore one or more flags; the people knew very well that those which did not show flags would have their windows broken.

On 9 November came a very special day. The NSDAP celebrated this date each year as the anniversary of Hitler's unsuccessful but nevertheless 'glorious' Beer Hall Putsch of 1923. Masses of people turned out for this occasion, which was always a full dress affair for the Nazis themselves. Disgrace attended any party official who failed to attend.

Tension mounted and with Germanic thoroughness the preparations were ticked off one by one. Party members knew what was expected of them because each had received a schedule from Nazi regional headquarters. The actual countdown began with Hitler's address to the nation, 48 hours before polling was to begin. Businesses were ordered to close and all civil servants, whether card-carrying Nazis or not, were instructed to attend at a stated hall to listen to the Führer's persuasive words. At 1 pm, siren signals brought the nation to a standstill, literally so, since transport ceased. Between 1.01 pm and 1.10 pm Josef Goebbels came to the microphone as a presenter for Hitler himself, who started speaking at 1.10 pm. When he finished, about 2 pm, the *Horst Wessels* march blared out and listeners joined in. Then, more sirens and back to work.

Election day was Sunday. By 9 am all Nazi Party members, each with family and friends, were in place to vote. This done, each man had duties. Some ensured that every house was flying the swastika while others toured the business districts to check on the enthusiasm with which traders filled their windows with swastikas. Yet more officials put into effect the order that all places of employment voted in 'closed ranks' by noon.

Newspapers throughout the nation carried advertisements to ensure that people understood 'the democratic process'. That is, they were told how to vote. The advertisement featured a specimen ballot paper with the injunction: *The circle under Nein should not be marked. When you have given your vote for Hitler and voted with Ja you will receive a button.*

The button was a brilliant idea in two ways. First it cost five pfennigs, providing funds for the Nazi party. Second, it ensured that every person had indeed voted. In every city, town and village, at railway and bus stations, at points of departure from the settlement, at the beerhalls were watch barriers or posts, where officials stopped any person not wearing a lapel badge. This individual would then be reminded of his 'democratic and patriotic duty' to vote. People who seemed reluctant were escorted to a polling station. Nazi officials were expert at spotting poll-dodgers.

The results of the two votes – for the NSDAP list in the Reichstag and for the plebiscite – were hailed as a triumph for democracy. For the plebiscite – 98.5 per cent voted *Ja*. For the NSDAP list, 98.5 per cent. But, then, the ballot paper carried no alternative list!

Why did some voters, if only a few, apparently vote against the proposals. This was designed to show that the system was honest – that people could show dissent. It might even have been possible that a few brave people did indeed vote as their conscience urged.

In terms of common sense the results were meaningless, but they clearly indicated that dictatorship ruled. The Nazis slavishly serving Hitler were in control and most ordinary people, for the sake of a quiet

Resting in the forest.

Standing beside his Mercedes, Hitler reads the daily press. Newspapers were sent to him by courier if they were not otherwise available where he happened to be.

life, simply did what they were told. Orders became more and more frequent and Nazi leaders at all levels of the organisation vied against one another to prove their ideological credentials.

The plebiscite had been so successful that the Nazis passed 'The Law on Plebiscites' on 14 July. It intended to use more of them to demonstrate at home and abroad the popular agreement between Hitler's dictatorship and the majority of the people. The Nazi heirarchy even believed in the validity of its majorities. It sometimes seemed, during the 1930s, that Western leaders and their peoples believed in them too.

The single party state was now a reality, and to such an extent that legal political activity was possible only within the NSDAP. The Führer State was born on 20 July 1933. The Reich Minister of the Interior, Frick, announced that the party system had now finished and the entire government of the German Reich was under the control of the Reich Chancellor, Adolf Hitler. The Hitler salute was to be used generally as the German greeting.

Despite Hitler's unimpeded progress there was a cloud on his horizon in the person of his old friend Ernst Röhm, the egotistical leader of the SA. Hitler had heavily depended on the SA as bullying enforcers and he had allowed Röhm to rise effortlessly through the councils of the Nazi Party until he was a member of the cabinet and a government vice-chancellor. But Röhm had ambitions to be more than a leader of uniformed thugs. He took the step – fatal as it turned out – of proposing to the cabinet that he be made minister of defence and, further, that he should be in charge of a new army that would be made up of the SA, the SS and the old army.

The army leadership was outraged. The Commander-in-Chief, General Walther von Brauchitsch, curtly announced: 'Rearmament is too serious a business to permit participation of peculators, drunkards and homosexuals'. This was the general army view of the SA and the SS. Hitler needed the army with him and in April 1934 he invited top service commanders on a cruise aboard the *Deutschland*. In this environment he did a deal with the generals and admirals: if they supported him in his proposal to become President in succession to the ailing Hindenburg he would muzzle the SA and leave the generals free to run the armed forces. They agreed – probably in the knowledge that Hitler planned to go much further than a mere muzzling.

At a stormy meeting with Hitler in June, Röhm backed down,

Last visit to Hindenberg before his death in July 1934.

The caption is misleading. Hitler paid his last visit in July but the old man died on 2 August. Hitler could feign any feeling but perhaps we may assume that he was sorry to see Hindenburg so close to death. Nevertheless, within an hour of his death Hitler announced that he was now both President and Chancellor.

promising that he would not attempt to overthrow Hitler by revolution. But according to Hitler, Röhm walked out of the room intent on doing just that. The SA was sent on leave and Röhm himself went to the resort town of Wiessee, near Munich.

Röhm and other SA leaders were to meet Hitler here on 30 June. Outwardly Hitler was calm, but in fact he was in near panic because of rumours that Hindenburg was about to turn over control of Germany to the army.

Heinrich Himmler, head of the SS, and Goering, who controlled a private army, joined Hitler in a plot. On the night of 29 June Hitler stayed at Bad Godesburg on the Rhine. Here he was told, as part of the plot, that Röhm and the SA were about to mount a putsch in Berlin and Munich. At two in the morning Hitler set off for Munich by air. He arrived two hours later, going straight to Röhm's hotel. Röhm was invited to commit suicide, and when he refused two officers shot him dead. The 'Night of the Long Knives' had begun. Before it was over more than 100 senior SA officers had been murdered. Vindictively, Hitler added General von Schleicher to the death toll. The previous year Schleicher, an old member of the Officer Corps, had sided with Röhm against Hitler. Hitler never forgave such 'disloyalty'. Equally he rewarded loyalty. Heinrich Himmler was told that his SS were now the enforcers of the Nazi Party.

The 'Night of the Long Knives' bloodily exposed the lengths to which Hitler and the Nazis were prepared to go, but there is little evidence to suggest that the Great Powers were making projections about future developments in Germany or developing contingency plans to deal with them. The foreign statesmen and their military chiefs, behaving like mice, seemed to be transfixed by the death adder of the Reich.

President Hindenburg gave Hitler a last great gift: his death on 2 August 1934. The old soldier died at the age of 94, and within one hour Hitler assumed total power over the Third Reich. In the afternoon and evening at ceremonies throughout Germany, servicemen took an oath of allegiance to the new Head of State and Supreme Commander:

I swear by God this holy oath, that I will render to Adolf Hitler, Führer of the German Reich and people, Supreme Commander of the Armed Forces, unconditional obedience, and I am ready, as a brave soldier, to risk my life at any time for this oath.

The people's day of mourning 1934: ceremony in Berlin State Opera House.

The 'people' pay their respects to the late President Hindenburg. For the first time, Hitler occupies the presidential box, which had earlier been the royal box. Despite his dislike for the system of monarchy, Hitler enjoyed his monopoly of the box and only Nazi leaders were invited into it, other than a few dignitaries and visiting foreign leaders. Hitler is third from left in the draped box.

Hitler was now able to keep his promise to the Army. He wrote to the Commander in Chief, von Blomberg: 'I shall always regard it as my highest duty to intercede for the existence and inviolability of the Armed Forces, in fulfilment of the testament of the late Field Marshal [*Hindenburg*] and in accord with my own will, to establish the Army formally as the sole bearer of arms of the nation'.

All this took place on the anniversary of the first day of German mobilisation for the Great War. Other Europeans may have forgotten that significant date but Hitler and his generals remembered it very well. Hitler's assumption of total power, the 'Blood Oath', his new accord with the armed forces and the date on which all this took place was an arrogant gesture to the world.

Hitler ordered another plebiscite, this time to gain the people's approval of him as President of the nation. Speaking from Hamburg on 17 August 1934, Hitler broadcast to the nation to explain the 'nobility' of his principles, and the same message appeared in every newspaper in the land.

> It is not for my own sake that I ask for this national vote, but for the sake of the German people. It is not I who require such a vote of confidence to strengthen and sustain me. It is the German people who require a chancellor supported by such confidence before the world. For I am nothing, my fellow countrymen, but your mouthpiece and I do not wish to be anything but the representative of your life and the defender of your vital interests.

This deprecation and apparent self-effacement, while actually stressing his overwhelming national and international importance, was Hitler at his most persuasive. The nation went to the polls in what some Germans called 'the Hitler vote'. It would be interesting to know what result a genuinely free ballot could have shown. What we have is a set of generally accepted figures. They show that 95 per cent of the people voted; 38 million of them, or 90 per cent, voted their approval. This left 4 million dissenters, but Hitler offered them no hope of a change of party or government. 'There will be no other revolution in Germany for the next one thousand years,' he said. This was the beginning of his 'Thousand-Year-Reich'.

He had more power than any Kaiser had known. He was head of

The Führer in front of the Imperial Palace at Goslar during the harvest festival of 1934.

Any occasion, even a harvest festival, was an excuse for the military to stage a parade. It was in this environment and amid soldiers that Hitler was relaxed. His own Heil Hitler salute was different from that of the people – hand held at right angles to the ground and palm open. He was not saluting so much as demanding attention. The question has often been asked – why was he so often bare-headed, even in uniform, and why did he carry his cap? The answer is – because every other military person of whatever rank had to keep his cap, hat or steel helmet on. Only Hitler himself could do as he pleased, but Goering and Hess were sometimes uncovered.

government, head of state and leader of the only party, and all soldiers and civil servants were personally sworn to him. The Hitler State was in being. The old formula that the monarch ruled by divine right gave way to a much more extravagant one – The Führer was the saviour appointed by Providence. Whatever else was guiding Germany it was not a *benign* Providence.

6

'A Right to Greater Living Space'

The German generals could see that Hitler's foreign policy was so belligerent that it would lead to war on at least two fronts simultaneously and this alarmed them.

For his part, Hitler developed a contempt for the generals whom he said were too timid. His resentment against them was fed by some of the senior Nazi officials, notably Heinrich Himmler, the failed chicken farmer who had risen to great power as head of the SS. A compulsive conspirator, Himmler told Hitler that General von Fritsch and his friends were planning to bring down the Nazi régime and restore the Kaiser to the throne. Hitler was ready to believe this untruth. Aiding Himmler in his plotting was his deputy, Reinhard Heydrich, a man in his own unsavoury mould. A former naval officer, Heydrich had been cashiered after the rape of a young girl and he hated the Officer Corps which he blamed for his disgrace. As head of the *Sicherheitsdienst*, the SS's sinister security service, and of the equally cruel Gestapo, Heydrich was in a position to do untold damage to his enemies.

Hitler spent the latter half of 1934 and much of 1935 gauging and testing world reaction to his plans. He had a few setbacks, but even they were instructive and enabled him to correct errors. For instance, a putsch he had authorised in Austria by local Nazis was abortive. On 25 July 1934, about 150 men falsely wearing Austrian Army uniforms broke into the Chancellory in Vienna and mortally wounded Chancellor Dollfuss. Over Austrian radio the plotters announced that Dollfuss had

Party Congress of Freedom: the youngest drummers of the nation.

These boys of Hitler Jugend excited the crowds at Nuremberg in 1935. Nazi instructors and propagandists had turned them into fanatical Nazis and when war broke out in 1939 they were a reservoir for the armed forces.

resigned and handed authority to them, but the Austrian army leaders were quick to move and the putsch failed. In Italy, Benito Mussolini was furious with Hitler's claim to Austrian territory and hurried his own troops into the Brenner Pass, ready to move into Austria should Hitler continue his aggression.

Hitler deferred his Austrian venture but approved the decision by General Ludwig Beck, army Chief-of-Staff, to increase the army's strength from 100,000 to 300,000. Hitler himself announced that in 1935 universal military training would be introduced. In the same speech he spoke about his fervent desire for peace.

Dutch shipyards were building U-boats for Germany, but foreign naval attachés in Holland swallowed the disinformation that they were destined for Spain. Dockyards in Keil, Wilhelmshaven and Hamburg were under tight security but why, if the only ships being built were 'improved 10,000 ton ships', as approved by the Versailles treaty? Actually, the pocket battleships *Scharnhorst*, *Gneisenau* and *Bismarck* were under construction, with other large ships.

The German League of Air Sports, under Goering's sponsorship, was flourishing and its members were turning up at events all over Europe. They professed keen interest in gliding and in racing planes. When Hitler became Supreme Commander, 250,000 German factories were engaged on war work. British Intelligence knew what was going on and alerted the Baldwin government but the cabinet reached what seemed to them to be a reasonable compromise. The British would accept German rearmament provided Hitler joined a general treaty guaranteeing peace in Europe. Of course he would!

And early in 1935 he peacefully took back the Saar basin from France. By using the plebiscite technique, the Nazis induced the people of the Saar to vote 10 to one for a territorial return to Germany. The Versailles provisions were going into reverse.

On Goebbels' advice, Hitler had been flattering the British journalist Ward Price of the *Daily Mail* by giving him exclusive interviews. This was in recompense for the support given to Hitler by Lord Rothermere, owner of the *Daily Mail* and one of many prominent Britons taken in by Hitler. Hitler now revealed to Price the true information that Germany was building an air force, a breach of the Versailles Treaty. The *Mail* made a major story of the news and the Nazis waited for official reaction. The British did not demur and while the French complained they took no action. The Nazi hierarchy was delighted, but they knew better than to gloat openly.

On 16 March 1935, Hitler decreed universal military service – as he had signalled the previous year. Now more than half a million men would be in uniform. What would the British and French do this time, he wondered? They remained passive, though on 11 April British, French and Italian foreign ministers met at Stresa to condemn Germany's violation of the Versailles Treaty.

What the Allies did not know was that on 21 May Hitler's 'Reich Defence Law' came into being, with Dr Hjalmar Schacht in charge of war production. While this law was secret, it was known in diplomatic circles that on the same day that it was passed the *Reichswehr* became the *Wehrmacht*, with Hitler as its supreme commander. The term *Reichswehr* referred to the army alone, that of the Weimar Republic days. *Wehrmacht* meant the entire armed forces. The change was more than one of mere nomenclature; it was an immense structural transformation.

General Werner von Blomberg was appointed minister of war and chief of the armed forces, while all three main armed services were given their own command structure. Such enormous changes could not be concealed, at least not from competent foreign military attachés.

Having put Germany on a nominal war footing, Hitler took the floor in the Reichstag on the night of 11 April and declared to the world that he wanted peace. ‘War is senseless, war is a horror’, he said. In a 13-point peace plan he called for ‘mutuality and reciprocity’ in mutual security, mutual disarmament, mutual trust. To the British he made a special offer – a joint British-German navy, with Britain contributing 65 per cent of the ships.

This was a transparent but nevertheless clever ruse to increase German naval strength, since at that moment it had less than 15 per cent of the British strength. *The Times* echoed the government’s response: Hitler had offered ‘reasonable, straightforward and comprehensive’ terms. In fact, Hitler’s aim was to split Britain from France and Italy, and by inducing the British to make a private deal this is what he achieved.

The Reich’s cabinet at the announcement of the Defence Law.

On Hitler’s right is Goering and second from left is Goebbels. The soldier is General Von Beck, Chief of the General Staff, 1934–38. At this cabinet meeting in summer 1934 Hitler announced a defence law that vastly increased the size of the army.

An historic meeting. Eden and Simon with the Führer.

Anthony Eden and the British Foreign Secretary, Sir John Simon, visited Hitler at the end of March 1934. (Eden became Foreign Secretary in December 1935.) He told them that a naval agreement might 'easily' be worked out between the two powers that would guarantee British superiority. Perhaps this is why Eden (seated on Simon's right) seems so pleased, but then Hitler's officials also seem happy. Hitler had set a bait for the British and they took it 'easily'. A dim-witted junior British clerk could have seen that by agreeing to Germany's possession of a navy as third as large as the British, the British government was giving Hitler authority to build a navy as fast as his shipyards could turn out ships.

Despite Hitler's triumphs and ever growing prestige, the nation's remilitarisation was slower than planned and his chiefs of staff cautioned him against pushing the British and French too far. The impatient Hitler ignored them and ordered three army divisions into the Rhineland on 7 March 1936, thus breaching the Treaty of Locarno. In the Reichstag, Hitler brandished defiance with his right hand while making peace gestures with his left. In remilitarising the Rhineland he was doing nothing more than meeting the wishes of the people who lived there, he said glibly. Further, to cover the nature of the operation Hitler pointed to its codename – *Winterübung* (winter exercise).

Von Neurath, the German Foreign Minister, summoned the British, French and Italian ambassadors and presented them with a document which contained a denunciation of the Locarno Pact – as well as far-reaching peace proposals. Francois-Poncet, the French ambassador, said sarcastically, 'Hitler struck his adversary in the face and as he did so declared, "I bring you proposals for peace!"' Hitler offered a pact of non-aggression to France and Belgium, valid for 25 years, and supplemented by an air pact to which Britain attached much importance.

The statesmen of Britain and France were so angry over the Rhineland grab that Hitler's generals took fright and urged him to pull out. Von Blomberg was fearful and frank: 'If Britain and France march together we cannot win a war at this time'. The Polish government offered military support to the French. Hitler, in agonies of doubt despite his bluster, anxiously read every communiqué from his diplomats in London, Paris and Warsaw.

The most welcome piece of paper was a telegram handed to Hitler at a railway station when his train was en route from Obersalzburg to Munich. It was a telegram from Edward VIII of Britain or somebody acting on his behalf and after reading the message Hitler said delightedly, 'The King of England will not intervene against me, he is keeping his promise. That means that all can now go well'. He may have been referring to a promise of support made by Edward when he visited Hitler at the Berghof as Prince of Wales. The story of the royal telegram is told by Edwin P Hoyt in *Hitler's War*, Robert Hale, 1988, p. 43. As Prince of Wales, Edward had earlier visited Hitler at the Berghof where he had congratulated the dictator on his 'stability'. Later, as Duke of Windsor, he corresponded with him, even as late as one month before the outbreak of the Second World War. Hitler regarded Edward Windsor as one of his finest 'trophies'.

Like Edward VIII, the British and French governments made it clear that they would not intervene over the Rhineland. Hitler, having faced down the great powers as well as his own cautious generals, was exultant. From that day Hitler was unchallenged in Germany and his reputation as a political strategist soared. His international reputation also reached new heights – and all because Britain and France had shown themselves to be irresolute. On that day, 7 March, the German troops were under orders to withdraw promptly should any immediate resistance be offered.

Later, Hitler said, 'We had no army worth mentioning. At that time it could not maintain itself even against the Poles. If the French had acted we would have been defeated in a few days. The air force we had then was ridiculous – a few Junkers and not enough bombs for them'. He was exaggerating the weakness of his forces but it was true that the British, French and Poles combined could have quickly overwhelmed the Germans.

On 8 March, France and Belgium called for the League of Nations to 'consider' Germany's Rhineland action, a futile proposal that caused laughter at the Berghof. The next day Poland secretly proposed to

After the New Year's reception of diplomats 1936.

Hitler rarely wore formal evening dress but his advisors had told him that it befitted his status as Reich President.

France that they jointly attack Germany. The French declined and the Poles concluded that regional alliances were useless.

Hitler now adopted his favourite ploy of the plebiscite to gain the approval of his people for his foreign policy, which was centred on the remilitarisation of the Rhineland and other renunciations of the Versailles treaty. Dissolving the Reichstag, he invited the Germans to pass 'honest judgment' on his programme, and at Breslau he made a keynote speech that must rank as one of the most forceful of his career.

For once opening his hands in the peace gesture – but only briefly – Hitler said:

> I appear before you as the peacemaker. All of us and all peoples have the feeling that we are at the turning-point of an age. Not we alone, the conquered of yesterday, but also the victors, have the inner conviction that something was not as it should be, that reason seemed to have deserted them. Peoples must find a new relation with each other, some new form must be created. Over this new order stand the words Reason and Logic, Understanding and Mutual Consideration. They make a mistake who think that over the entrance to this new order there can stand the word Versailles. That would be the gravestone of the new order, not its foundation stone.

The stated poll results of 29 March 1936 were:

Qualified voters	45,453,691
Votes Cast	45,001,489 (99 per cent)
Votes against or invalid	540,211
Votes in favour of the Nazi list	44,461,278 (98.8 per cent)

Whatever the authenticity of the vote it was evident to all foreigners in Germany and to all observers that Hitler had never been more popular among his people.

Paradoxically, the real losers over Hitler's Rhineland coup were the German General Staff. Von Blomberg – 'an hysterical maiden' according to Hitler – and his colleagues had so vehemently opposed *Winterübung* that its subsequent success made them look foolish. Even more, it made Hitler seem like a political and military genius. It was from this time that Hitler believed in his intuition and his generalship. On 9 March, the War Minister had summoned Hitler's military adjutant three times to order him to pass on to the Führer the perilous nature of the Rhineland adventure. Now, all dangers passed, Hitler mocked the generals. To rub in this mockery he promoted von Blomberg to be the first Nazi field marshal and Werner von Fritsch, army chief of staff, to colonel general. A French military attaché stationed in Germany reported to Paris that as the German generals continually opposed an aggressive foreign policy, so Hitler became more wedded to it.

By failing to challenge Hitler's coup in the Rhineland, France was signalling that it was not prepared to defend the elaborate security system it had built up since 1918. Similarly, the Baldwin government in Britain was signalling that its support for France was minimal and that the British would not fight to uphold a treaty. This was how Hitler and most of Europe read the political lessons of the Rhineland seizure. It was now a question of who next would Hitler threaten.

Hitler always worked on a broad front in foreign policy and with Goebbels' assistance he planned a propaganda campaign built around the Olympic Games of 1936. In winning the games for Berlin, Goebbels had pulled off an international coup; now he used the games to show a regenerated and re-invigorated Germany, liberal and lively, a country of song and friendship for all. For the duration of the summer of 1936, with many thousands of foreigners touring Germany, the Nazis suspended their anti-Jewish campaign. No longer were there *Jews Not Welcome* signs at the entrance to every public place, anti-semitic cartoons and articles did not disfigure the press and Jewish performers appeared on the Reich's concert platforms.

Visiting foreigners were spectacularly fêted and one night Goebbels and his wife Magda entertained more than 1,000 guests. Goering also staged great parties. Every individual who might have caused trouble was locked up or banished to the country. Attractive young men and women were assigned to act as guides and interpreters and they duly impressed the foreign guests, whose general impression was that Hitler's Germany was a good country to live in and that Hitler himself was a liberal, progressive ruler. The only unfortunate note occurred when the American negro sprinter Jesse Owens won gold medals. The Nazis could not hide their racist anger and contempt but the incident was important only to the more thoughtful witnesses to it.

Taking over of the Reichführerschule in Bernau in January 1933.

Hitler established a military-type training school where men could be taught his principles of leadership not merely in warfare but in economics, administration and Party management. The foundation stone for the school was laid in this field.

With the Olympic Games over and milked for all they were worth, Hitler intensified his political programme, internally and abroad. Even before the summer ended Germany signed a pact with Austria, promising not to interfere with that country's internal affairs. Simultaneously, but in secret, the Nazi party in Austria was guaranteed important seats in government. Hitler also sent aircraft and artillery to support the fascist Franco forces in the Spanish civil war, though he was more interested in prolonging the war than helping Franco to win it quickly.

That October, Hitler inveigled the braggart and easily-duped Mussolini into signing a treaty with Germany in what became the Rome-Berlin Axis. Only a month later Germany and Japan signed an anti-Comintern treaty, further obvious preparation by Hitler towards war.

Meanwhile the German forces kept on growing and as a direct consequence unemployment fell to zero; those people who were not in the forces were making the hundreds of thousands of pieces of equipment for the forces. Great public buildings were appearing all over the country, but especially in Berlin, which Hitler wanted to rival Rome and Paris in grandeur.

In November 1937 Hitler laid out before five key Nazi officials his plan for Germany in the next few years. The identity of those men in

On the new Alpine road.

Hitler was fascinated by roads and it was he who built the famous autobahns. His chief of great projects was Engineer-Doctor Fritz Todt, standing next to Hitler. Organisation Todt employed vast numbers of slave workers on military projects.

itself indicates the thrust of the Führer's thinking. They were Blomberg, minister of war; Fritsch, army commander-in-chief, Raeder, chief of the navy, Goering, chief of the Luftwaffe and von Neurath, Reich Foreign Minister. Their leader spoke for four hours but the essence of his plan can be summarised briefly. (My words)

Germany has a right to greater living space (*Lebensraum*) than other nations. Our foreign policy is to enfold, enlarge and protect the entire German racial community, no matter where Germans might live in other countries. Space is paramount. Britain and France are both hate-inspired and will oppose Germany and will have to be fought but they will not fight over Czechoslovakia,

which, with Austria, we will annex. Germany will no doubt have
to fight Russia too but this is no great problem.

Hitler's men had studied *Mein Kampf*, so the plan was not new to them,
but the specificity startled them and they raised objections and diffi-
culties. Hitler raised his voice and rode over them. For three months
in 1938 he was preoccupied with sexual and social scandals, real or
manufactured, involving Blomberg, Fritsch and others but in March,
after further bullying and plotting, he moved towards the annexation
of Austria.

The political situation in Britain and France helped Hitler enor-
mously. British politics were in disarray over Chamberlain's
appeasement of Mussolini, who was hungrily developing an empire in
North Africa. Anthony Eden, the Foreign Secretary, resigned in protest
over British inaction. Chamberlain knew what was happening in Berlin
and Vienna because his ambassadors were keeping him informed. He
was aware of the ultimatum that Hitler had given Chancellor
Schuschnigg that Germany would invade unless the Austrian government 'invited' German troops into the country to 'avoid bloodshed in
Vienna'. Chamberlain treated the affair as a minor administrative matter. Referring to a meeting in Berchtesgaden between Hitler and
Schuschnigg, he said, 'What happened at Berchtesgaden was merely
that two statesmen agreed upon certain measures for the improvement
of relations between their two countries'.

The sophistry implicit in this comment is breathtaking and Hitler
was happy; he knew now that Britain would not act against him.

Neither would the French, since in Paris there was no government
at all. The country was leaderless, and although a caretaker foreign ministry was in being it was powerless to act. The French armed forces,
without a political head, were impotent.

The invasion of Austria took place on 11 March and four weeks later
the triumphant Hitler invoked yet another plebiscite. This time the
German and Austrian people together would vote on the *Anschluss*, the
union of Austria with Germany.

No secret ballot was considered necessary and when the farce of
counting was complete the Yes vote in Germany was 99.09 per cent and
in Austria 99.75 per cent.

The pogrom against the Jews began at once and it was more vicious

The Führer lays the foundation wall of the meeting house in the Adolf Hitler Centre.

The Centre was for the study of Nazi ideology. Hitler was immensely interested in architecture and buildings, especially those in the grand Gothic style. He built them for the greater glory of himself, though he constantly stated that they were for the glory of Germany and its people.

than that in Germany, with many Austrian Nazis appointed to important positions. Hitler now had 7,000,000 more people, together with Austria's resources. In London, Chamberlain told the House of Commons, 'Nothing could have arrested what actually has happened in Austria unless this country and other countries had been prepared to use force'. But it had been obvious for years that only force or assassination would stop Hitler.

While the Nazis went systematically about the business of cowing and coercing Czechoslovakia, they invited British and French military officers, and some from other countries, to Germany to witness displays and manoeuvres by the armed forces. They were calculated to show the guests that German military might was truly formidable. The Nazis used various ruses to delude the foreign officers into believing that

Germany was even stronger than it was. For instance, the Luftwaffe had limited numbers of Me109 and Me110 fighters but they were 'multiplied' by moving them from one airfield to another ahead of the shepherded guests. The British should have known about these tricks because they had been employing similar tactics to deceive German attachés in Britain.

Some of Hitler's senior generals were so worried about his mania for conquest and what they regarded as his irrationality that they conspired to overthrow him. They proposed to allow him to order the invasion of Czechoslovakia and then arrest him for trial before a 'People's Court'. General Beck was an active conspirator and even the new chief of staff, General Halder, approved the scheme, while staying aloof from the plotting. The anti-Hitler generals made only one precondition: the British and French must support them by intervening if Hitler moved against Czechoslovakia. It was not much to ask. On a special trip to London, General Ewald von Kleist-Schmenzin, who had British friends, asked the government, through Sir Robert Vansittart, chief diplomatic advisor to the cabinet, to announce that Britain would take military action should Germany attack Czechoslovakia.

Winston Churchill told Kleist that he was certain Britain and France would stand firm – but he was not in government. Prime Minister Chamberlain called the British ambassador home for consultations, but his advice was that Chamberlain should meet Hitler face to face. This was agreed to. When Hitler received the message that the British PM was coming to Germany he said mockingly, 'Heaven has fallen on me!'

Poor Chamberlain, a lamb among wolves! The British people believed that their leader's mission was to tell Hitler where to 'get off'. But it was Hitler who did the talking and after a tirade he suggested in reasonable tones that if the Sudetenland – the German-speaking area of Czechoslovakia – were to be conceded to Germany the Czech problem might be solved. He promised, with the air of a man making a great concession, that he would refrain from military action at least until he and Chamberlain spoke again. It was now 15 September and the Czech operation was planned for 1 October, so the Führer was giving away nothing.

Meeting in London, the British and French statesmen agreed to partition Czechoslovakia on the basis that everywhere inhabited by more than 50 per cent Sudeten Germans would go to Germany. No Czechs were present at this fateful meeting, and when they did learn the details they naturally objected. The British told them they had no alternative but to accept and that Britain could do nothing further for them. The harried President Benes turned to the Russians, who assured him that they would honour the treaty but, so sorry, there was a difficulty which the Czechs would find in the fine print of their treaty: *Russia could help the Czechs only if the French did so too*. Alas, the French had repudiated the treaty.

On 22 September, Chamberlain and Hitler met in Bad Godesburg, on the Rhine, where Hitler and the Nazis had earlier done much devious plotting. Hitler came to the point: Germany must occupy the Sudetenland at once. He did not admit it to Chamberlain but he and his cronies actually wanted to have a short decisive war, one just long enough to demolish the Czech army, and to frighten the other armies of Europe.

At a further meeting on 23 September Hitler told Chamberlain flatly that his troops and administrators would take over the Sudetenland on 28 September. When Chamberlain refused to countenance this ultimatum Hitler, changing to his reasonable mode, pointed out that the paper he held was not an ultimatum at all but a mere memorandum: it was even stamped memorandum – see for yourself. However, as a concession, Germany would delay moving until 1 October.

Day of the Armed Forces, Nuremberg 1935. Motorised heavy artillery.

For the first time since the war, genuine German military might was on display and the crowd was delirious with delight. Hitler is to the forefront above the draped swastika.

Saying that he was pleased with the 'relation of confidence', the desperate Chamberlain departed. British and French public opinion now swung in favour of the Czechs, who declared that they would fight alone. In the showdown that followed the British and French governments agreed, without grace and without warmth, to back Czechoslovakia. Events moved quickly, Hitler agreed to 'concessions'. On 29 September, British, French and Italian diplomats met the Germans in Munich but now the Führer's 'concessions' turned out to be demands for even larger tracts of Czechoslovakia. This was a Hitler technique, in matters small and large:

Agree to 'concessions', shake hands on the deal and then introduce new and crippling conditions, together with the threat of punitive action if they were not met. It so outrageously wrong-footed the other side that it always worked.

In the early hours of 30 September 1938 the British, French, Italian and German negotiators signed an agreement, without consulting President Benes or any other Czech official. *It called on Germany to march into Sudetenland on 1 October and occupy it.* This was treating Czechoslovakia as a hostile, recalcitrant country when it was in fact an ally of the West. President Benes, to save the inevitable slaughter of his troops, ordered the army not to fight. Prime Minister Chamberlain boasted that he had much to be proud of; he had achieved peace in his time. But in the House of Commons Winston Churchill stripped away Chamberlain's puerilities and presented the reality: 'We have sustained a total, unmitigated defeat. We are in the midst of a disaster of the first magnitude. All the countries of middle Europe and the Danube, one after the other, will be drawn into the vast system of Nazi politics. And do not imagine that this is the end. It is only the beginning'.

The appeasers of the House of Commons shouted him down.

7

The Nuremberg Rallies – Blood and Honour

Many leaders of the democratic and civilised nations who made no attempt to stop the Nazis' rise to power claimed ignorance as a mitigating circumstance for their shameful passivity. 'How could we have known Hitler's intentions?' they asked. This book explains how they *could* and *should* have known.

Some statesmen proffered whole lists of excuses for their inactivity covering the years 1919 to the late 1930s. These are some of them:

- They had not realised that Germany was rearming.
- Hitler seemed more like a political buffoon than a serious threat to international peace.
- It was reasonable to assume that the Nazi Party would have a short but violent life.
- The Nazi Party and Hitler were political freaks, a phenomenon so unusual that nobody could be expected to know how to deal with it.
- Many Western politicians exculpated themselves by saying that as they did not know the German language they could not be expected to comprehend the dangerous nature of what Hitler was telling the Germans.

All these claims to be regarded as innocent parties could be quickly demolished. One activity of the Nazi Party under Hitler's personal leadership and encouragement was vividly evident and completely comprehensible to anybody who viewed the newsreels of the 1920s and 1930s. And most people did. The picture houses provided what television stations disseminated after the 1950s – documentary news in depth. Among the most enthralling events in the entire world were the Nuremberg rallies, the Nazis' most successful means of arousing the Germans' emotions and channelling them to heights of passion that left the people mere creatures in the Nazis' fantasy world.

The annual mammoth party rallies at Nuremberg, celebrating the Party Day, were like a gigantic national pulse beating with the disturbing insistence of a drum. They had an hypnotic quality even to those of us who saw them only in black and white on a screen. For the participants – and every German participated in one way or another – they were intoxicating.

From the beginning the Nazis' rallies were a potent mixture of theatre and propaganda, of colour and ritual, of symbolism and insignia, of banners and bands, of crowd manipulation by talented ringmasters. The first true rally was in 1923 but the swastika or *Hakenkreuz* (hooked cross) made its appearance before that. In the years 1918–19, German troops came upon it in Finland. The Erhard Brigade painted it on their helmets when they marched into Berlin during the Kapp putsch in the spring of 1920. It is probable that Hitler saw it in his youth as a symbol of the anti-semitic DNSAP, the German National Socialist Workers' Party, which was actually an Austrian party.

Hitler himself designed the black swastika in a white circle on a red background. It was he who chose the basic red – the revolutionary colour – because he knew it would provoke the Left, who claimed red as their own. Red was also important as the blood colour; Hitler was constantly talking about blood in one way or another.

The symbolism of Hitler's choice of Nuremberg for the great rallies was obvious – this was the city that had been host to the pageants of the Holy Roman Empire. The discipline of the time and the symbolism of the military trappings – such as the eagle standards – fascinated Hitler.

The rally held in the autumn of 1923 was a positive step in the development of the party as a strong political power. It was a demand for public attention and for serious recognition by the government and all other parties. At this and at all his first mass meetings, Hitler brought forward the most extreme ideas of National Socialism – anti-semitism, the annexation of all German-speaking territories, the

Party Congress 1934. The consecration of the standards.

This was a slow task since Hitler himself 'blessed' each standard. The atmosphere was always thick with emotion during a consecration.

political destruction and if necessary the physical destruction of all enemies of National Socialism.

Hitler invariably closed the rally with a final address which was guaranteed to be dynamic. For instance, at the end of the 1929 rally he chose as his theme the deterioration of German national power. He pointed out that the Spartans secured their strength by rigorously selecting the strong and developing a healthy society. As individuals and as a society, Hitler wanted the Germans to be Spartans and he returned to this theme time and again.

From 1929–30 Goebbels introduced the dynamic 'Heil Hitler!', first as a greeting for the Führer, then as a form of adoration, finally as a battle cry. 'Heil Hitler!' came readily to people's lips as they raised their stiff arms, fingers pointing forward, in salute. Goebbels had cribbed the salute from the Italian Fascists, who used it when saluting Mussolini. No gesture in history so swept a race of people as the raised arm for Hitler to the thunderous chorus of 'Heil Hitler' and later 'Sieg Heil!'.

Goebbels' inspired handling of Nazi Party propaganda was dramatically illustrated in the way that he exploited the death of Horst Wessel, a name that became known throughout the Party and the armed forces. Wessel was a young Berlin SA leader who in 1930 was shot and killed during a brawl in a harlot's bedroom. He was an unsavoury individual, a bully and a rapist, but he had written a simple marching song. Goebbels raised it to the status of a national anthem and turned Wessel into a hero. The Horst Wessels song – often simply referred to as *the* Horst Wessels – was adopted as the official Nazi Party song and it became the second official anthem, after *Deutschland Über Alles*. The *Horst Wessels* was sung at public meetings and was used in the musical background at the Nuremberg rallies.

To celebrate their rise to power the Nazis planned to make Party Day 1933 the grandest ever. Hess suggested its title, the Party Day of Victory. The organisation needed to manage the huge event is probably best shown by a selection of statistics. The largest tented camp had tents so huge that each one held 400 men. On one side of the camp was a row of monster field kitchens of brick construction, with immense ovens and boilers, that produced countless gallons of soup. The camp for the Hitler Youth was similarly equipped with 600 boys sleeping in a tent, in rows of 10 tents.

More than 250 special trains brought 400,000 party members to

Nuremberg. Six hundred reporters were given special permission to attend the various congress functions, including 200 foreign correspondents; another 3,000 reporters were registered to attend Party Day but without access to the indoor meetings. Every foreign writer arriving at Nuremberg railway station was addressed in his own language by a uniformed interpreter and assigned to his hotel room, where he found waiting for him his identity card, programmes and Nazi Party brochures. Here, too, he met his own personal guide.

The high point of the first session on 1 September 1933 was Julius Streicher's reading of Hitler's proclamation to the delegates, which on this occasion damned the influence of Marxism in Germany. The proclamation credited the Nazis with having overcome treason and perjury and with restoring faith, honour and decency in Germany.

The following day two spectacles in particular showed the Nazis' talent for theatrical events on the grand scale. One was a review in which 160,000 high party officials and their followers took part. The leaders stood in rows divided by a wide middle avenue, with three narrow lanes on either side. Waves of flag bearers had been concealed behind a long embankment at the rear of the field. Now, at a signal, they swept forward, marching 12 abreast and with banners high. The effect of the colour, the discipline and the movement was emotional in its intensity. Hitler arrived to be greeted by his uniformed followers on the parade ground and by the 100,000 spectators in the stands. Their shouts of acclamation were thunderous.

The second impressive spectacle took place in the afternoon when 60,000 boys from Hitler Youth paraded in rows in the Youth Stadium. They represented another 1,500,000 Hitler Youth who had not been lucky enough to win selection for attendance at Party Day. Each boy carried a knapsack and a blanket roll on his shoulders and each carried in a sheath a long knife with the engraved inscription *Blut und Ehre* (Blood and Honour). During ritualistic ceremonies the youngsters kissed the blade's inscription.

The boys mounted their own banner march before Hitler appeared. The cheering and saluting from the boys lasted a full 10 minutes before the Führer could make himself heard.

On the afternoon of the final day a march past took place in Nuremberg's splendid town square, with Hitler standing in his car to

The Führer with Hitler Youth at the party congress 1935.

When standing in his car as it carried him the length of every row of youth on parade, Hitler reverted to the standard official salute. He never wore service medals or decorations other than the Iron Cross First Class, which had been conferred for bravery in the first world war. In the car are Rudolf Hess and Baldur von Shirach. It would be interesting to know what was amusing them but we can be sure that they had not made a joke about their boss.

watch the parade. The *New York Times* correspondent graphically reported the event:

> Unceasingly and apparently tirelessly until almost dusk a stream of the well-knit, athletic youths passed their leader, fading away down

the street in a blare of brown caps and grey knapsacks. They moved by battalions, 500 strong and 12 boys to the file. As the flags swept by, a forest of swastikas almost a block long for each regiment, every flagstaff was wreathed with the green oak leaves of victory and every cap bore a flower or a knot of green. Young Germany was showing its strength. And young Germany is very strong.

This is one of the songs of Hitler Youth groups on the march or in camp:

Germany, thou will gleaming stand, even though we should go under
Forward! Forward! resounds the heroic fanfare. Forward! Forward!
Youth knows no hazards. Be the goal ever so high,
Youth will yet achieve it.
                    Chorus
Our flag flutters before us, as into the future we move man for man,
We are marching for Hitler through night and through danger, with
the flag of youth for freedom and bread,
Our flag flutters before us.
Our flag is the new time and the flag leads us into eternity.
Yes, the flag is greater than death!

The attention given by the Nazis to the lighting of rallies on Party days is significant because it emphasises the leaders' profound preoccupation with operatic effects. To illuminate the field for night ceremonies, 150 huge spotlights were installed; they consumed 40,000 kilowatts of electricity during one evening. The long stretch of Greek pillars in the background were illuminated by 1,200 spotlights. Another 50 powerful *Klieg* lights were positioned to light the grandstand, the speaker's platform, the flagpoles and the field itself. The illumination was so bright that the reflection in the sky could be seen as far away as Frankfurt. The firework displays as a rally finale were great crowd pleasers. In one such display a swastika appeared in the evening sky, surrounded by green leaves and crowned by a huge eagle.

The 1933 rally showed that the Nuremberg Rally as an institution had become extremely important in the life of the German nation, or the Third Reich as the Nazis were calling it. The word Reich means empire; the first Reich was that ruled over by Frederick the Great in the 18th century; the second Reich was the one created by Kaiser Wilhelm.

In linking himself to these two great German kings, Hitler increased his status immeasurably.

The Nazi leaders deemed the 1933 Nuremberg rally so successful that they organised a full week's activities for 1934.

For Party Day in 1934 the Labour Service participated in a party congress for the first time. Its members consisted of 'graduates' from the Hitler Youth and from more than 1,000 labour camps scattered throughout Germany 52,000 representatives had been selected to attend the rally. At noon on 8 September the spade-carrying columns began their formal progress past Hitler and his chieftains in an amazing display of show marching. American reporter William Shirer described the sheen of the sun on 50,000 polished blades, with the columns of men standing to attention, bare-chested in one long ceremony. They broke into chants of ideological slogans, and their goose-stepping brought more spontaneous cheering from the spectators than did the marching of the Stormtroopers. Hitler told the men of the Labour Service that the spade was 'a gun of peace'.

National Labour Day 1 May 1934. A Youth demonstration in the Berlin Lustgarten.

The Führer leaves after his long oration. Hitler was often tired after a taxing speech but the mass acclamation seemed to recharge his energy.

Hitler Youth is front of the Brown House before ceremonial admission into the Party.

The palatial Brown House, in Munich, was the national headquarters of the Nazi Party. In the last days of the Weimar Republic the Brown House had been the offices of a state within a state. Note the girls from the League of German Maidens marching at the left of the boys.

But this was by no means all that the rally organisers offered in 1934. En masse, more than 200,000 men took an oath of allegiance to Hitler, who was then driven slowly back into Nuremberg. The procession was 10 miles long, with torch bearers 12-abreast bringing up the tail of the column. A reporter for *Völkischer Beobachter* painted a word picture of the spectacle. 'The torch parade, seen from a hill above the city, looked like a river of molten bubbling lava which slowly finds its way through the valleys of the city.'

In a speech to Hitler Youth, Hitler said:

We want to be a peace-loving people but at the same time courageous. We want our people to be honour-loving; to that end, from earliest childhood you must learn the conception of honour. We want to be a proud people and you must be proud to be the youthful members of the greatest nation. We want an obedient people and you must learn to practise obedience. We want a people that is not soft but hard as flint and we want you from early youth to learn to overcome hardships and privation.

From their cheers and clapping the crowd made clear their approval of Hitler's commands, for that is what his words were.

The last day of the week-long rally belonged to the army, which took over the enormous parade ground known as the Zeppelinwiese. For the first time since the Versailles Treaty the German people witnessed their army in exercises and what they saw was new, exciting and dramatic. Machine-guns and naval mine-throwers were shown in action and a communications battalion – a unit new to the armies of Europe – went about its work while a commentator described it. In the great arena, artillery, motor-cyclists and cavalry gave the crowd the excitement they were craving. According to William Shirer, who was there, it was difficult to exaggerate the frenzy of the 350,000 spectators. The foreign military attachés, though less demonstrative, were equally impressed. As always the week's activities ended with banners, bands and beer.

For Party Day 1935 the Nazis allotted much of an evening to women and in Congress Hall Hitler was introduced by Frau Gertrud Scholtz-Klink, head of the National Socialist Women's Organisation. In his remarks on the role of women in the new Germany, Hitler sounded yet another implicit warning to the non-German world; indeed, it was almost explicit in what it prophesied. His comments were blatantly chauvinist and sexist but German women were accustomed to that. Their Führer told them that the Third Reich was breeding a generation

Reich Party Day 1935: The Labour Soldiers.

Spades shining bright, resplendent in their military style uniforms, 90,000 men of the Labour Service parade for their Führer. Hitler called the spade 'the gun of peace' but the Labour service men were taught how to handle conventional personal weapons as well.

of men who, because of their vigor and strength, would be more attractive to women. As proof of the new masculinity, he referred his audience to the muscles of the Labour Corps men. 'You are the mothers of the nation', he told the women, emphasising that the nation rewarded women who had five children or more. They would wear with pride the 'Mother's Cross', a decoration in gold and blue enamel. When women were not actively child-bearing they were 'the eternal companions of men in work and battle'. The women applauded him when he said, 'We men are willing to fight but when we are wounded you must nurse us'. He concluded with his well-worn assertion that the highest triumph for women was to bear and tend babies.

From several photographs in this book and from newsreels of the Hitler period, it is obvious that German women were excited in Hitler's presence. Despite his lack of any obvious sex appeal he had an extraordinary attraction for women of all ages. From his early days in the Party he was well aware of his power over women. He told his friend Ernst Putzi Hanfstaengl:

> Someone who does not understand the intrinsically feminine nature of the masses will never be an effective speaker. Ask yourself what a woman expects from a man. Clearness, decision, power and action. What the Party needs is to get the masses to act. Like a woman, the masses fluctuate between extremes. The crowd is not only like a woman but women constitute the most important element in an audience. The women usually lead, then follow the children and at last, when I have already won over the whole family, follow the fathers.

Hanfstaengl produced this recollection during an interrogation carried out by the US Office of Strategic Services in 1946. He is quoted in *Eva and Adolf*, by Glen Infield, London 1975, page 22.

This was akin to what Hitler had written in *Mein Kampf*:

> Like women who would rather yield to a strong man than dominate a weak one, so the masses love a dominator better than a supplicant and feel inwardly more satisfied by a doctrine which tolerates no other beside itself than by granting of liberal freedom.
> *Mein Kampf*, German edition, page 292.

National Socialism was that doctrine.

According to Hans Peter Bleul, an observer on the scene in Germany:

Women hung eagerly on every word of Hitler's speeches. It was sexual excitement which he knew how to handle, especially among his female listeners, just as it was an erotic affinity with all the elements of passion and ecstasy which characterised his relationship with the masses, whom in any case he identified with womankind.

Sex and Society in Nazi Germany, London, 1973, page 46.

In 1937 Hitler spoke to an audience of 20,000 women and ended with one of his most dramatic assertions: 'What have I given you? What has National Socialism given you? We have given you man.' Otto Strasser, a veteran Nazi who was present, said that the reaction from the female audience was 'comparable only to an orgasm'. (Otto Strasser, *Hitler and I*, London 1940, page 81.)

In this way German farmers greet their Führer, Adolf Hitler. Bückeberg 1935.

There is nothing feigned and nothing forced about the ecstatic delight these people show towards their Chancellor-President. The girls are wearing their traditional scarves to show their respect, and the SS soldier from the Death's Head regiment is more interested in gazing at his Leader than in keeping back the crowd.

The Army of Labour. Reich Party Day 1935.

It was always an exciting moment for Hitler, as he mounted the steps at Nuremberg parade ground to address the countless thousands of 'Warriors' of the Labour Corps. The banners were inflammatory, the acclamation overwhelming.

Most women granted a personal interview were enchanted by Hitler's manners, charm, electrifying blue eyes, caressing voice and attentive remarks. In private he was polite and considerate and he was said to be patient and understanding to his secretaries and female staff. However, in public he could be foul-mouthed and abusive to women who opposed his political views. There could have been few who took this risk.

Many women were profoundly affected by the sexually dominant image that they saw in Hitler. According to numerous reports, young women lined the road leading to the Berghof, or 'eagle's nest', and screamed hysterically when Hitler was driven past. Some ripped open their blouses to expose their breasts to him. Members of the BDM (the German Maidens' League), naked beneath their uniforms, lay in wait to offer themselves to him. Female patients in hospital invoked the

Führer's name before being anaethetised for operations while others cried 'Heil Hitler!' as they gave birth and asked that their babies be at once shown a picture of the Führer; this was not difficult since all institutions were adorned with his image. Such reports proliferate from many sources during the 1930s and they must be given some credence. Their significance in what they revealed about the political face of the Third Reich was not studied until 1944, when the US government commissioned a psychoanalytical study. It was at least 16 years too late.

Otto Strasser's observation that there was something orgasmic about the reaction of an audience of women to a speech by Hitler could be applied to the general public's reaction to the newly reorganised and re-equipped army which Hitler exhibited in September 1935.

Having totally repudiated the limitations imposed by the Treaty of Versailles, the army now had on display the latest armoured cars, a tank battalion, mechanised artillery batteries, an anti-tank company and anti-aircraft guns. Fighter aircraft and heavy bombers took part in the exercises that followed the static display and foreign military observers estimated that 100,000 troops were involved. A naval detachment from an officers' training school appeared and was given a huge roar of approval. That day Hitler was not so much showing off his country's might as brandishing it. Most significantly of all, the medal struck for Party Day 1935 showed a bust of Hitler flanked by a steel-helmeted soldier and a capped SS soldier.

During Party Day 1936 – given the name of Party Day of Honour and Freedom – 90,000 men of the Labour Service carried out another party ritual. The battalions 'presented spades' as a military drill and then stood to attention. A full-bodied voice from a loudspeaker resonated over the great field: 'Once a year the spade shall rest. Once a year comes for us a time to stand before our Führer, for whom we work day by day. In this hour, new faith is kindled'.

Ninety thousand voices responded, 'We are ready'.

There followed the *Horst Wessels*, after which the prompt-voice announced, 'No one is too good . . .' The men, hands grasping spade grips, completed the sentence '. . . to work for Germany'.

'No one is too humble . . .' came the prompt, and again the response '. . . to work for Germany'.

'Each has the right and each has the duty' followed by 'to work for Germany, the Fatherland'.

A new voice picked up the ritual: 'We have carried you [*Hitler*] deep in our hearts but we cannot say it in words'.

'Germany! Fatherland!' was the swelling response.

Voice: 'Then the law came, work became duty. Now we all stand side by side'.

'Germany!' 'Fatherland!'

'The fulfilment of duty for us is not serfdom. We carry the spade in the service of the nation. We come before you [*Hitler*] as workers.'

'Germany! Fatherland!'

'The Führer wants to give the world peace.'

The Labour Service troopers responded, 'Wherever he leads we follow!'

After another emotion-binding song the first voice sounded again across the field. 'We lift up our heads and think of our brothers who suffered in the trenches and of the others who fought murder and hatred in the streets. They died for Germany.'

'Today we can live for Germany!' intoned the 90,000-voice choir.

We will probably never know whether or not the language of this ritual and its implications were studied by British, French and other 'experts'. But even at a superficial level of analysis the Labour Service performance at Nuremberg in September 1935 indicated an attempt to shape a religious ritual or a cult. The Nazi manipulators were trying to find a substitute for Christian worship, which they abhorred. Hitler, the Führer, is a god creature, the object of a 'new faith'. Once again there is emphasis on the sacrifice of the trench generation, though neither here nor in any of the other attempts to forge a psuedo-religion is there recognition that Germany was largely responsible for the war that caused such suffering. Konstantin Hierl, chief of the Labour Service, addressed the men after the ritualised service to express, he said, the pride the men felt in marching and performing for the Führer. The Führer himself spoke to the assembled 90,000 stalwarts and as always recited his long list of Nazi achievements since the Party's assumption of power.

Every element of presentation at the 1935 rally and those that followed sought to show Hitler in a mystical light. In 1936 the culmination was Hitler's appearance before 140,000 *Gauleiters*, the regional chiefs, who were waiting in the gloom of the Zeppelinwiese. First came a roar of cheers from outside the arena, stage-managed to build up expectation

Party Congress 1935. Consecration of standards and honouring of the dead.

This is one of the best views ever taken of the great parade field at Nuremberg. Backed by his senior colleagues, Hitler harangues an audience of a million people. Immense and complex organisation was needed to get them into place and to disperse them after the ceremonies, and all without the slightest disorder. The Führer wouldn't have liked that.

within. Hitler appeared as a lone silhouetted figure at the top of great marble steps. After a pause, 150 army searchlights placed low down shone out like 'spears of light' – to quote an observer – which picked out the Führer. Brightly lit, Hitler, in his brown uniform, proceeded down the steps to meet a group of dignitaries waiting for him. As massed bands played, Hitler led the procession across the field to the podium, which he ascended. Then he waited for silence; he understood the value of silence that crept up on a vast crowd. On this occasion Hitler was not at that moment preparing to speak but pausing for the next amazing moment in the ceremony. Far in the distance and glowing mystically in the light from thousands of spotlights appeared what looked like an advancing wall of blood. In fact, the redness came from 25,000 banners of Nazi organisations from all parts of Germany.

Specially selected bearers of the Nazis' national colours marched with this disciplined horde for a time, then moved ahead of it to thrust through the vast crowd of brown-clad men. In the narrower lanes these flag-bearers marched six abreast, but down the broad central avenue they moved 20 abreast. 'It was a great tide of crimson seeping through the blocs of brown,' said an observer. It was blood symbolism, beloved of the Nazi leadership.

While this was happening, less powerful searchlights perched on the rim above the grandstands were angled down onto the arena and picked out the gilded eagles on the standards. The final effect, which was truly beautiful, was of red flecked with gold.

Never before had Hitler seemed more like a spiritual being, a deity whose wisdom could not be questioned, yet a mortal who could achieve miracles. The emotion of that evening was so intense that it bound those present to Hitler without qualification; few Germans could have had any mental reservation. The many foreigners present must have been impressed and surely some of them realised that *this* nation under *this* leader would be virtually impossible to defeat in war. They had seen within the previous few days the astonishing strength of the new German army.

The 1937 and 1938 Nuremberg rallies were bigger than that of 1936 and in their military content even more awesome. The other European powers were shown exactly what they would be facing in the event of a great war. The Luftwaffe unveiled the first modern helicopter as well as aircraft that could take off and land at a mere 30mph from an area not much larger than a suburban lawn. Bombers and fighters not previously seen in the West excited the interest of military attachés – and filled some of them with foreboding. The 1936 Nuremberg Rally should have sounded the alarms of impending war.

While the rallies at Nuremberg were the great propaganda events of the Nazi calendar, many other rallies were held all over Germany, by states, districts, cities and towns. It was easily possible for the enthusiastic Nazis of any age to attend public events every weekend, indeed every day during the warmer months. Ordering 100,000 Hitler Youth to kiss their *Blut und Ehre* dagger blades at a Nuremberg Rally was splendidly impressive, but Hitler and his manipulators knew that if those boys were to use their daggers to spill an enemy's blood and win honour for themselves they had to be put through this performance many times. Ultimately, every part of a rally ritual, from its logistical preparation to its orgasmic climax, was rehearsal for war. Did the rest of the world see it merely as a concert?

After the success of the 1938 Nuremberg Rally another gigantic event was planned for 1939 and 1,000 special trains were ordered, more than ever before. But before that came Hitler's 50th birthday on 20 April 1939. Again, the celebrations were on a colossal scale with loyal demonstrations all over the nation. Without doubt the most significant event was the military parade through Berlin. The armed forces column stretched for 250 kilometres, or 150 miles, and even then, for various

Buckeberg 1934.

This was one of the relatively smaller Party parades of the year.

reasons, many units did not take part. This was no phony parade given artificial length by large gaps between formations and by moving trucks, tanks, guns and motorised troops in a great circle and taking them past the saluting base twice. This display of Hitler's military might was genuine, and the foreign military attachés who witnessed it were awed, as the Nazis meant them to be.

Having hardened the German people and softened up the world, Hitler, his lieutenants and the Nazi Party generally were ready to put history back on course with Germany it its rightful place as leader and exemplar. The Nuremberg rallies had been dress rehearsals, demonstrations and morale-builders.

The time for the reality of *Blut and Ehre* had arrived and the 1939 Nuremberg rally did not take place. Hitler needed those 1,000 trains for the invasion of Poland. The date was 1 September 1939.

Conclusion: Unheeded Warning, Untold Suffering

So it is quite clear that Hitler warned us in messages that were simple, perfectly understandable and often dramatically illustrated. His warnings came over and over again in his own words and those of his chief lieutenants, and in films and photographs that were shown all over the world. His cruel racial policies, his expansionist ambitions, his belief in and love of war were all openly displayed throughout the 1920s and 1930s.

Why then did the leaders of the Western nations and the Soviet Union, who were to pay for their inaction with the slaughter, suffering and destruction of the Second World War, do almost nothing about it? How could they possibly have believed Hitler's protestations that he was a man of peace? Why did they not stop his march to conquest and tyranny? Could they have done so? I believe that they could and many other people have made attempts to answer these still burning questions. The answers are not the subject matter of this book.

But what we can no longer tolerate is the pathetic excuse that 'we didn't know', that we were not warned. Certainly Hitler could have been stopped militarily up to 1937; he admitted this himself.

It is probable that Britain and France did not try to stop him then partly because of fear of Communism, against which Hitler appeared to stand as a bulwark. He presented himself as the West's champion

against 'the Reds'. Other factors that inhibited the Great Powers – as they still were – included the almost universal revulsion against the trench warfare and slaughter of the First World War and a determination not to repeat it. Internal economic problems and political divisions and jealousies between the Powers also got in the way of concerted action against the spread of Nazism. The Soviet Union was in the throes of Stalin's internal terror and unready to fight Germany.

In the end, and virtually to his own timetable, Hitler carried out, with increasing speed and unmitigated brutality, what he had promised the German people he would do. These promises were warnings to us which, until it was too late, we chose to ignore. Hitler counted on it.

In retrospect, what gave Hitler his power over Germans has been best expressed by one of his inner circle, Baldur von Shirach, leader of Hitler Youth. Twenty-two years after the war, Shirach wrote in very different language from that he had used in 1936 when he had extolled Hitler's qualities (see pp. 24–27):

> The German catastrophe was not only caused by what Hitler made of us but by what we made of Hitler. Hitler did not come from outside; he was not, as many see him today, a demoniacal beast who seized power by himself. He was the man the German people wanted and the man we made master of our own destiny by our own unrestrained glorification of him. For a Hitler only appears in a people which has the desire and the will to have a Hitler. It is a collective failing in us Germans that we give honour to men of extraordinary talents – and nobody can deny that Hitler had these talents – and arouse in them the feeling that they are infallible supermen.
>
> *Ich Glaubte an Hitler*, Hamburg, 1967.

It wasn't only the Germans with a 'collective failing'. We suffered from it too. Our collective failing was a paralytic passivity in the face of supercharged and evil aggression.

Mourning ceremony for Field Marshal von Hindenburg in the court of honour of the Tannenberg Memorial.

Hindenburg's coffin was in pride of place but Hitler, at the dais, was more prominent during the ceremony. 'I will bring even more honour to the Fatherland than my friend von Hindenburg did', said the Führer, the new President.

Index